For Orla

from

olfe

# The True Meaning
of
Christ's Teaching

*Translated from the French*
*Original title :* LE VÉRITABLE ENSEIGNEMENT
DU CHRIST

# Omraam Mikhaël Aïvanhov

# The True Meaning
## of
# Christ's Teaching

*2ⁿᵈ edition*

**Collection Izvor**
**No. 215**

EDITIONS  PROSVETA

Prosveta S.A. – B.P. 12 – 83601 Fréjus Cedex (France)

ISBN 2-85566-322-9
édition originale : ISBN 2-85566-289-3

# TABLE OF CONTENTS

*The reader will better understand certain aspects of the lectures published in the present volume, if he bears in mind that Master's Omraam Mikhaël Aïvanhov's Teaching is exclusively oral.*

# 1

# "OUR FATHER WHICH ART
# IN HEAVEN..."

*The Lord's Prayer*

*Our Father who art in heaven,*
*Hallowed be thy Name.*
*Thy kingdom come.*
*Thy will be done,*
*On earth as it is in heaven.*
*Give us this day our daily bread.*
*And forgive us our trespasses,*
*As we forgive those who trespass against us.*
*And lead us not into temptation,*
*But deliver us from evil.*
*For thine is the kingdom,*
*and the power, and the glory, for ever.*

*Amen.*

In the course of his teaching, Jesus taught his disciples a prayer which has been recited by Christians everywhere, ever since, and which we know as the Lord's Prayer, or Our Father. Contained in this prayer is a very ancient science handed down by a tradition which had existed long before Jesus' time. But it is expressed in such a condensed, encapsulated form in the Lord's Prayer, that it is not easy to grasp the full depth of its meaning.

An Initiate goes about things in the same way as Nature. Take a tree, for instance: the whole tree: roots, trunk, branches, leaves, flowers and fruit are all miraculously condensed in a pip or a seed. The marvel of a tree with all its potentiality to live for years and years and constantly produce fruit in spite of the buffeting of wind and weather, is all there, in that one little seed buried in the soil. And this is an image of what Jesus did: he condensed all his sacred science into the

Lord's Prayer hoping that it would take root in the souls of those who recited it and meditated on it and that, as it grew, they would gradually discover the untold grandeur of all it contains: the tree of Initiatic Science.

All Christians, everywhere, recite this prayer, whether they be Catholic, Protestant or Orthodox. But they have not always understood it correctly. In fact quite a lot of them think it is not rich nor eloquent enough. They have composed their own, far more impressive, poetic, all-embracing and – let's face it – interminable prayers... and they find them highly satisfactory! Yes, but what do their prayers really contain? I am afraid that if you analyse them you will not find very much. So, let's try and see what is hidden in the words of the Lord's Prayer... although I must say at the outset that it is so immensely rich, we shall never be able to explain it all.

"Our Father which art in heaven"

A Creator and Lord of Heaven and earth and of the whole universe exists and his dwelling place is heaven. But heaven, in the Jewish tradition, has several different regions and each region has its name: Kether, Hokmah, Binah, Hesed, Geburah, Tiphereth, Netzach, Hod, Yesod and Malkuth. Each heavenly region also has

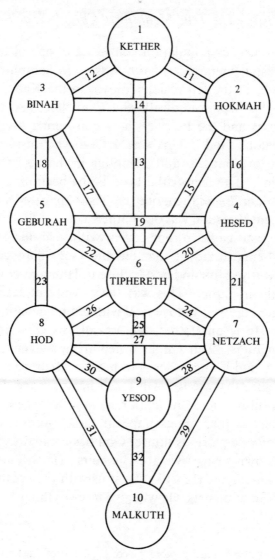

Sephirotic Tree

a numerous population consisting of one of the celestial hierarchies, from Angels to Seraphim. Here, in the ten regions known in the Kabbala as the Sephirot, dwells the God described by Moses and the Prophets as a consuming fire, a "jealous God". This was a God who inspired not love but fear and trembling in the hearts of men: "The fear of the Lord is the beginning of wisdom". And then, one day Jesus appeared and taught that God was our Father.

Jesus came to replace fear with love. Instead of being afraid of that terrible God, man can now love Him and nestle close to Him as a child with his father. This was the novelty of Jesus' teaching: we can love God with tender devotion, for He is our father, we are all His sons and daughters. "Our Father which art in heaven".... Yes, and if our father is in heaven, then we can be sure that we too will reach heaven: one day the father and his children will be together. There is marvellous hope in these words: the hope of a glorious future. God has created us in His own image; we are His heirs; He will give us kingdoms, He will entrust us with the organization of planets, He will give us everything.*

* Chapters 2 and 3 explore the consequences of this notion of man as son of God in greater detail.

"Hallowed be thy name". God has a name which we must know before we can bless or "hallow" it. Christians are not accustomed to calling God by name, they just call Him "God", but Jesus was heir to an ancient tradition and he knew that God has a mysterious, unknown name. Once a year, when the High Priest uttered God's name in the Holy of Holies, in Jerusalem, his voice was covered by the sound of trumpets, drums, flutes and cymbals, so that the people gathered before the Temple would not hear the sacred Name. In the Old Testament this name is given as Yahveh (Yahweh) or Jehovah and we know only that it consists of four letters: Yod, He, Vau, He: ה ו ה י*.

Kabbalistic tradition teaches that the Name of God is composed of 72 names or powers and it might help you to understand this better if I tell you how the Kabbala explains it. Each letter in the Hebrew alphabet is identified with a number and as Yod י = 10, ה = 5, ו = 6 and ה = 5, the four letters add up to 26. When the Kabbalists write the Name of God in a triangle they place the letters like this:

* Hebrew reads from right to left.

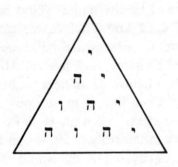

Another way is this:

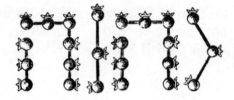

When the Name is written in this way, the 24 Knots represent the 24 Elders mentioned in Revelation and each knot has 3 fleurons giving a total of 72.

But what does it mean to "hallow" or sanctify God's name? Don't be surprised if I begin by calling to mind the four elements: earth, water, air and fire, of which the world is made. There is a connection between the forces and virtues of the four elements and our bodies, hearts, minds, souls and spirits, and each element has its own presiding Angel. This is why, when an Initiate wants to purify himself he asks the Angel of earth to absorb all the impurities of his physical body, the Angel of water to wash his heart, the Angel of air to purify his intellect and the Angel of fire to sanctify his soul and spirit. Blessing or sanctification, you see, corresponds to the highest level, that of the soul and spirit, the level of fire and light.

The notion of holiness has always been associated with the notion of light. The Bulgarian language contains a good example of this: *svetia* in Bulgarian means holy or saint and has the same root as *svetlina*, light. A saint (*svetia*) is one who possesses the light (*svetlina*): all is light within him, he shines and radiates light. And as you know, traditional art has always depicted a halo of light surrounding the heads of the saints. Holiness is an attribute of light, of the pure light which shines in the spirit.

Only that which is pure can purify; only that which is holy can sanctify. Only light, therefore, can sanctify, because only light is holiness. It is in the purest light of the spirit that we must bless and sanctify God's name. A name represents, resumes or contains the entity it designates, so that if we are infused and penetrated by the holiness of light when we utter the name of God, we have the power to draw Him into ourselves and into everything around us, to sanctify all objects and all living creatures. It is not enough to go to church and repeat: "Blessed by thy name", we must bless His name really and truly within ourselves. If we do this we shall know the extraordinary joy that comes from having the power to illuminate whatever we touch, whatever we eat, whatever we look at.

Yes, the greatest of all joys lies in really grasping what this means and every day, everywhere, in blessing, sanctifying and radiating light on all that comes our way. Then, only, are we doing what Christ told us to do. If all we do is to repeat "Hallowed be thy name" and never actually do anything to bless that name in the way we live our daily lives, it means that we haven't understood the first thing about it. When we say or write the name of God we ally ourselves to divine forces and we can actually draw these forces down into the physical sphere. But this work has to begin in the mind. "Hallowed be thy name". To hallow God's name is a work of the spirit and it takes place, first and foremost, in our minds.

"Thy kingdom come...." From this we see that the Kingdom of God does exist and that it has its own laws, and its own harmonious organization. To imagine what it is like is totally beyond us! But we do seem to get a fleeting glimpse of it every now and then in our purest, most spiritual moments, but it is only at these special times that we can begin to have any idea of what the Kingdom of God means. It is no use relying on our experience of earthly kingdoms, with all their disorders, conflicts and madness, to guide our imagination. It is possible to establish the Kingdom of God on earth; there is a whole body of teaching and methods to bring this about. But it is not enough to ask for it in our prayers. The trouble is that we have been asking for it for the last 2 000 years and it still has not come because people do nothing to make it come.

With this second petition, "Thy kingdom come", we have moved from the domain of the mind and spirit to that of the heart. God's name must be hallowed in our minds but it is in our hearts that His Kingdom must come, for the Kingdom of God is not a place but a disposition or attitude which reflects all that is good, generous and disinterested. Two thousand years ago Jesus said that the Kingdom of God was at hand: this was true for some, but for most people it still has not come and it never will, even in another twenty thousand years, if we are content to wait for it to come from the outside and do nothing about the inner reality. For some, then, the Kingdom has already come; for others it is coming, and for yet others it will come one day, but who knows when!*

We come now to the third petition of the Our Father, one that is even less well understood than the others: "Thy will be done on earth as it is in heaven". The whole of Initiatic Science is summed up in those few words. In Heaven God's will is always carried out without a murmur, because His servants are totally attuned to it. Amongst human beings this is not the case and that is why Jesus gave us this prayer, so that we should learn to adjust our own wills to the will of God. There are all kinds of comparisons we could use to express this idea: a mirror for instance, which faithfully reproduces the object it reflects, or any electrical appliance. Every electrical appliance is built on the principle of the two, complementary poles: the emissive pole on the one hand and, the other, the receptive pole which has to tune in and adjust itself to the emitter. The emitter is Heaven and the receiver is the earth, material creation. The task of the material world is to attune its vibrations and even its physical forms to those of Heaven, to conform to the qualities and virtues of Heaven so as to manifest here, on earth, the splendour which exists on High.

* See Chapter 4: "Seek ye first the Kingdom of God and His Justice".

The mission of mankind is to work in the world and cultivate it so that it becomes a beautiful garden of flowers and fruit, a dwelling place for God... and, instead of that, what do people do? Well, I know many who say, "Oh, you know, the earth doesn't really interest me anymore...." Of course, this simply shows that they have not understood Christ's teaching. And yet, surely, it is clear enough. He says "May thy will be done, on earth as it is done in Heaven." Everything is already perfect in Heaven, it is here, on earth, that there is still a lot to do. So we have to come down to earth, consciously and deliberately, and be ready to take risks and get involved with material things. This is the only way to conquer the material world and bring it life, the life of the Spirit : for the life of the Spirit has yet to be made manifest on earth as perfectly as it is in Heaven.

It is up to us, Christ's workers, to put our shoulders to the wheel. It is not enough to repeat this prayer and then live in such a way as to prevent it from being granted. We often do that ; we are like someone who says, "Come in, come in" and then slams the door in your face. We mutter a prayer and then : "Bang", we close the door. It is amazing how people can be so unaware of what they are really doing... and then they go and boast that they're Christians !

"Thy Will be done on earth as it is in heaven" : in these few words are contained the whole of theurgic magic. If the disciple understands the awe-inspiring impact of this prayer, if he manages to make it come true, one day he will be a transmitter, a mirror in which Heaven is reflected, he will, himself, be a Heaven. That is what is written into this prayer; that is what is expected of us.

The first request : "Hallowed be thy name", concerns our minds. In order to hallow and bless God's name, we must study, meditate and fill our conscious minds with light. The second request : "Thy Kingdom come", concerns our hearts, for God's Kingdom can only come into hearts full of love. The third request touches our wills. "Thy Will be done on earth as it is in heaven" implies hard work, obstacles to be overcome, victories to be won, and for all this, strength and perseverance are needed. That is why we have to train ourselves and learn to work with methods which can help us to harmonize with Heaven and vibrate on the same wavelength. What do you think we go and see the sunrise for? So as to become like the sun, of course ; so that the earth, our earth, our physical bodies, shall become like the sun. When someone is attuned to the sun and spends time in loving contemplation of it, he becomes luminous, and radiates warmth and life like the sun. So you see, our custom of being present at the sunrise is a very practical method for making this request of the Lord's Prayer come about. It is one method... and there are plenty of others.

There is nothing more important for man than to apply himself to doing the will of God, because to do so is powerful magic. As soon as you decide that you are going to do only God's will your whole being is "occupied", set apart for God and closed to all other influences, and the forces of opposition which wanted to use you for their own ends can no longer do so. This is the only way to safeguard your purity, strength and freedom. If you are not occupied by the Lord you may be sure that you will be occupied by others and will end up by being at the beck and call of all manner of self-serving, anarchical wills which will ultimately be your downfall.

"Our Father which art in heaven, hallowed be thy name, thy Kingdom come, thy will be done on earth as it is in heaven". There is a hidden meaning in each of these requests, a meaning that can be discerned only by someone who has a profound grasp of reality. When archeologists examine ancient manuscripts or monu-

ments and artifacts, they see the texts or objects
and the plans and disposition of the old build-
ings as relics which can give them some idea of
that era and of the mentality of the people who
left them. Thanks to these clues they can pen-
etrate their intentions and have some idea of
what they meant. And we can do the same: we
can look on the prayer Jesus bequeathed us as a
sort of monument, a testament to be studied and
dwelt on until we uncover the vast teaching concealed in it.

The first three requests of the Lord's Prayer
correspond to the three principles in man: the
mind, which must be full of light in order to illu-
mine and make all things holy; the feelings or
heart, the central powerhouse which must become God's Kingdom, the Kingdom of peace
and of love for all creatures; and finally the will
which corresponds to the physical dimension in
which, by our acts, we have to express and reflect all that is in Heaven. Isn't that marvellous?
To my mind no other activity can compare!
When we have done our part, God will take care
of us and give us all the rest... but what else can
He possibly give us? We shall have received
everything. Once we understand what these
three requests contain we realize that we already
have it all: light, since we understand; happiness, since we love; health and strength, since

we are working, and accomplishing something.
What else could one possibly want?*

"Give us this day our daily bread". This is
the first of the three requests which directly concern man himself. The first three concerned the
Lord (we always have to begin with God): to
know and bless His name; to seek His Kingdom
and to do His will. Now man asks for something
for himself and his first request is for bread. Why
bread? Because bread is the symbol of all the different kinds of food we need for our existence.

The bread Jesus is talking about is certainly
not just material bread. In the Gospels, spiritual
nourishment is mentioned far more often than
physical food. For example, when the Devil
challenges Jesus to change stones into bread, he
replies: "Man shall not live by bread alone, but
by every word that proceedeth out of the mouth
of God." At another time he says: "Blessed are
they which do hunger and thirst after righteous-
ness." It is true, of course, that he multiplied the
loaves and fishes to feed the multitude, but later
he told that same multitude: "Labour not for
the meat which perisheth, but for that meat
which endureth unto everlasting life...." The
spiritual significance of food becomes even more

* See Chapter 5 "On Earth as it is in Heaven".

evident at the Last Supper, when Jesus blessed the bread and wine and gave them to his disciples, saying: "Take, eat; this is my body" and "Drink ye all of it; for this is my blood." And again, "Who so eateth my flesh, and drinketh my blood, hath eternal life."

Man's first supplication for himself, then, is for bread, the daily bread he needs to sustain life, but this need is even more poignant on the spiritual plane: someone who does not take some spiritual food every day, dies.*

"And forgive us our debts as we forgive our debtors." This is a better translation of the Gospel text than "forgive us our trespasses" for every breach of the law is like a dishonest act by which we incur a debt we are going to have to pay back. If, for example, someone abuses another's love and trust, it is a form of theft and, one way or another, he is going to have to pay back what he has taken dishonestly. The idea of karma is based on this truth: that we have to come back to this earth in order to pay for transgressions committed in previous incarnations.... Someone who has paid off all his debts need not reincarnate.

* See Chapter 6 "He who eats my flesh and drinks my blood shall have eternal life."

But whether we ask to be forgiven for our sins or released from our debts, the idea at the heart of this supplication is that of forgiveness. And this was new: for the first time in the history of mankind Jesus introduced the notion of a merciful God, a God who forgives. The God of the Old Testament was portrayed by Moses as a vengeful God who delighted in exterminating sinners: those who were guilty of transgressing the law were punished without mercy. And although the gods of some other religions were less vindictive, no one had ever insisted on the mercy of God in the way Jesus did. The notion that God forgives is a logical consequence of the very first words of the Lord's Prayer: "Our Father". God forgives us for the simple reason that a father always forgives his children.

We must not forget, though, that Jesus added, "As we forgive our debtors." Unfortunately, as we do not release others from their debts nor forgive them their offenses, the Lord does not release us from our own debts. Nor does he forgive us our sins. If we want to be forgiven we have, first of all, to forgive. The notion of forgiveness is central to the Christian religion.*

* See Chapters 7 and 8: "Father forgive them for they know not what they do" and "Unto him that smiteth thee on the one cheek offer also the other".

Jesus' teaching was one of love, whereas the founders of the other major religions put more emphasis on justice, wisdom, knowledge or power. Of course it is true that Buddha taught compassion but nowhere will you find a doctrine of love of such breadth and such clarity as that of Jesus: in this he was unique. And that is why he was crucified.

When Jesus associated with social nobodies or even criminals and prostitutes he was flouting all the existing conventions. No one had ever seen anything like it: people who, by rights, should have been stoned were his friends: he visited them, ate with them, accepted their invitations. And that is why those who were determined to maintain the existing social order could not accept him. When they realized that he was revealing the most sacred truths to the poor and uneducated they decided he must die. Jesus was crucified because, when he revealed a religion of love, he broke down the age-old barriers which others had an interest in maintaining.

"And lead us not into temptation, but deliver us from evil...." You will certainly be shocked if I tell you that I am not at all sure that what Jesus really said was: "lead us not into temptation..." but I will explain why, in a moment.

For the time being, let's be content to note that in spite of this prayer we are continually subjected to temptation... even Jesus was tempted. Saint Matthew says: "Then was Jesus led up of the spirit into the wilderness to be tempted of the devil." If the Holy Spirit led Jesus into the desert to be tempted we must conclude that it was necessary: Jesus had to be subjected to these temptations. In the desert the Devil taunted Jesus, saying: "If thou be the Son of God, command that these stones be made bread." Later, setting him on the pinnacle of the temple, he said: "If thou be the Son of God, cast thyself down: for it is written, He shall give His angels charge concerning thee: and in their hands they shall bear thee up, lest at any time thou dash thy foot against a stone." And finally, having taken Jesus up into a high mountain, he showed him all the kingdoms of the world and said: "All these things will I give thee, if thou wilt fall down and worship me."

The Devil made these three propositions to Jesus for a very precise reason: as I have already explained, they correspond to the three levels in man: the physical, the astral and the mental. But what is far more interesting is the answer Jesus gave to each one, for they show us that if we want to resist temptation we have to know how to answer the tempter, what arguments to use against him. When someone replies to his suggestions with irrefutable arguments he realizes that he will be unable to seduce him and leaves him alone.

This is something you must realize: it depends entirely and only on you, whether or not you agree to be influenced. Even the Devil cannot force you against your will. Of course, if you have no discernment and do nothing to protect yourself, you are liable to be swayed. The spirits of evil are very skilful at presenting you with all kinds of appetizing bait and then, as soon as you take it, you are hooked and gradually, very gently, they will drag you under and destroy you. God has given them the power to do this, but only if you are weak and ignorant. Once you have been drawn into their orbit, once you have taken a step in their direction their power is tremendous: they can tear you to pieces... and it is your own fault. It is you who are guilty. They are only being themselves and doing what they are allowed to do: tempt you. That is their job. But why do you have to be so stupid as to let them snare you in the first place?

Yes, if the forces of evil destroy a man it is because he has allowed them to do so. It all depends on him: if he refuses to let them in to take possession of him they are powerless. Their power comes from the fact that they manage to fool him into thinking that if he does thus and so he will be stronger, richer or happier. If he succumbs to their enticements they can get a grip on him and destroy him. But if he remains steadfast they are powerless to harm him. So one could say that man is as powerful as God, but only when it is a question of saying "No", of rejecting, resisting any attempt to influence him. When it is a question of imposing his own will and getting what he wants it is much more difficult; his possibilities are very limited and it takes a lot of time and hard work. But when it comes to saying "no" man is all-powerful. Hell itself can do nothing to him against his will. If he lets himself be swayed it is through ignorance: he is not aware of his own strength.

In some countries – Turkey, for instance – they have a special wrestling technique: the wrestlers are almost naked and their bodies are oiled, so it is almost impossible to get a hold on an adversary: he slips through their hands like an eel. Well, that is how we should behave when we are confronted with a bad influence. If you say "no" to the spirits of darkness it is as though you were "oiled" and they cannot get a hold on you. But if you have bits of string and all kinds of loose ends hanging round you – symbolically speaking – then they can get a grip on you and you will never shake them off. They will truss you up and throw you to the ground. So, leave no loose ends for undesirable entities to hang on to, be so slippery that they cannot get a grip... and to be slippery means to be capable of saying "no".*

When you find yourself faced with temptation say to yourself: "Of course, it's a very attractive idea, really enticing, but it's not for me! I intend to become a man of wisdom, a Son of God. I'm not going to be led astray, I shall overcome this temptation. I'll be stronger than it is." And, above all, do not look on temptations as a handicap or an obstacle in your path. On the contrary, use them to stimulate you and make you stronger. A man of wisdom, an Initiate, never tries to avoid temptation, in fact he sometimes contrives it on purpose in order to acquire greater self-control. Someone who runs away from temptation is bound, sooner or later, to give in. You cannot solve problems by running away from them.

So now you will have understood why I doubted that Jesus really said, "Lead us not into temptation." We need to be tempted in order to measure our true capabilities and become stronger. When we are tempted it is like having a problem to solve or an exam to pass: it makes us

* See Chapter 9 : "Watch and Pray."

put our best foot forward and show what we are
capable of. So we should not pray to be spared
temptation, only to be capable of resisting. Evil
and the forces of evil exist and it is useless to ask
the Lord to wipe them out: he won't do it. In the
Book of Revelation it says that it is only at the
end of time that the Beast will be cast into a lake
of fire and brimstone. Until then we shall always
be up against evil, so we had better learn the
right attitude to take in order to deal with it.

And now let's look at the final verse of the
Lord's Prayer: "For thine is the kingdom, and
the power, and the glory, for ever." In order to
understand these words we must turn our attention to the spiritual regions I mentioned earlier;
to what Jesus called "the heavens" which correspond to what the Kabbala calls the sephiroth.
The ten sephiroth together form the Sephirotic
Tree or Tree of Life. The name of each sephirah
expresses a quality or attribute of God: Kether,
the crown; Hokmah, wisdom; Binah, intelligence; Hesed, mercy; Geburah, strength; Tiphereth, beauty; Netzach, victory; Hod, glory;
Yesod, the foundation; Malkuth, the Kingdom.
The tenth sephirah, Malkuth, reflects and sum-
marizes all the others. (See diagram on p. 34)

Jesus said that the Kingdom of God was like
a mustard seed. A seed always represents a beginning, the beginning of a plant or a tree. But

# THE TREE OF LIFE

1 Ehieh
Kether – *The Crown*
Metatron
Hayot Ha-Kodesch – *Seraphs*
Reschit Ha-Galgalim – *The first vortex (Neptune)*
♇

2 Iah
Hokmah – *Light*
Raziel
Ophanim – *Cherubim*
Mazaloth – *The Zodiac (Uranus)*
♅

4 El
Hesed – *Mercy*
Tsadkiel
Hachmalim – *Dominations*
Tsedek – *Jupiter*

3 Jehovah
Binah – *Wisdom*
Tsaphkiel
Aralim – *Thrones*
Chabtaï – *Saturn*
♄

5 Elohim Gibor
Geburah – *Force*
Kamaël
Seraphim – *Powers*
Maadim – *Mars*

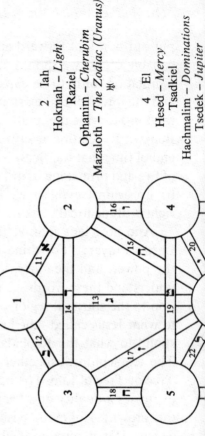

7  Jehovah Tsebaot
Netzach – *Victory*
Haniel
Elohim – *Principalities*
Noga – *Venus*  ♀

6  Eloha ve Daath
Tiphereth – *Beauty*
Mikaël
Malahim – *Virtues*
Chemesch – *Sun*  ☉

8  Elohim Tsebaot
Hod – *Glory*
Raphaël
Bneï-Elohim – *Archangels*
Kohav – *Mercury*  ☿

9  Chadaï-El-Haï
Yesod – *The Foundation*
Gabriel
Kerubim – *Angels*
Levana – *Moon*  ☽

10  Adonaï-Melek
Malkuth – *The Kingdom*
Sandalfon
Ischim – *Perfect Men*
Olam Iesodoth – *Earth*  ♄

we must realize that although, on the physical
plane, all our beginnings are below, the situation
is reversed on the spiritual plane: on this level
everything begins on high. And this is why
growth on the physical plane is an upward
movement, whereas on the spiritual plane, it is a
downward movement. The seed of the Tree of
Life, therefore, is Kether, the first sephirah.
When the seed begins to grow it divides into two
before putting out a trunk, branches, leaves,
buds, flowers and fruit; and the fruit, in turn,
produces more seed. When the seed, Kether, is
planted, it becomes a tree as it passes through
each sephirah in turn all the way to Malkuth.
The ripe, life-bearing fruit, the flesh given for
our nourishment, is Yesod and this is the fruit
that produces the seed: Malkuth. So you see
that at the end of its cycle of growth the seed that
was first sown becomes the seed in the fruit and
Malkuth, the seed below is identical to Kether,
the seed above, for the beginning and the end of
any one thing are always identical. Every new
departure is the conclusion of an earlier development and every conclusion is a new departure
for further development. Everything has a beginning and an end and yet there is no such thing as
an absolute beginning. Every cause produces its
effect and each effect becomes a new cause pro-
ducing a new effect.

In the final phrase of the Lord's Prayer, "For thine is the Kingdom, and the Power and the Glory," Kingdom, Power and Glory correspond to the three sephiroth: Malkuth, Yesod and Hod.

The Kingdom is Malkuth, the Kingdom of God, the realm of realization, and this is the planet Earth.

The Power is Yesod which means "foundation" or basis, because this is the sephirah which reigns over purity, the true foundation of all things. Sexual energy is associated with Yesod because true power, the life-force, is expressed in sexual energy. It is this same power, on a higher plane, which gives rise to all great achievement. The planet associated with Yesod is the Moon.

The Glory is Hod, the bright light of knowledge and science. Its planet is Mercury.

So this last phrase of the Lord's Prayer means: "Thine are the three regions which represent the final stages of Kether's growing into Malkuth; the three regions which represent the realm of realization." The Kingdom, the Power and the Glory form a triangle, a repetition of the first triangle: "Hallowed be thy Name, thy Kingdom come, thy Will be done." The Name, the Kingdom and the Will are Kether, Hokmah and Binah. So the upper triangle: Kether, Hokmah and Binah, which represents creation in the invisible, spiritual world, is reflected in the triangle below: Malkuth, Yesod and Hod, which represents formation, realization on the physical level. The phrase "for ever and ever..." corresponds to the Sephirah Netzach which means "eternity."

Now, perhaps you are wondering where to situate the remaining Sephiroth: Tiphereth, Geburah and Hesed. You should be able to find the answer for yourselves if you work out the correspondences using the same method and with the explanations I have just given you. But let's refer to the Our Father again and take it in order, starting with the fourth verse: "Give us this day our daily bread." Our true daily bread, the inexhaustible source of life is the light flowing from Tiphereth, the Sephirah ruled by the Sun, for it is from the sun that man receives both physical and spiritual nourishment.*

"Forgive us our debts as we forgive our debtors." This request corresponds to the Sephirah Hesed and when we say these words we are creating a bond with Hesed. Jupiter, the symbol of benevolence and generosity, is the planet which corresponds to Hesed. In order to pardon others we have to have that sovereign assurance

---

* See Chapter 6: "He that eateth my flesh and drinketh my blood hath eternal life."

we find in Jupiter that no one can ever rob us of the riches God has in store for us.

"Lead us not into temptation but deliver us from evil." This verse represents Geburah with its corresponding planet, Mars. It was the angels of Geburah who banished Adam and Eve from Paradise after they had been tempted by the serpent, for they have the special task of combating evil and impurity of every kind. When you establish a bond with Geburah you become stronger, more able to resist evil.

Now, if you look at the diagram (p.40) you can see how these sephiroth can be grouped into triangles: the upper triangle, formed by Kether, Hokmah and Binah, corresponds to the sublime world of emanation which the Kabbala calls Atziluth. Below this comes the inverted triangle of Tiphereth, Hesed and Geburah which corresponds to the world of creation, or Beriah. And still lower comes the triangle formed by Yesod, Hod and Netzach which corresponds to the world of formation, Yetsirah. Finally Malkuth which, as I have said, is a condensation of all the other sephiroth and which corresponds to the world of realization, Asiah.

Malkuth is the Kingdom; Yesod the Power; Hod the Glory, and Netzach Eternity. So when you say, "For thine is the Kingdom, and the Power, and the Glory, for ever", you create a

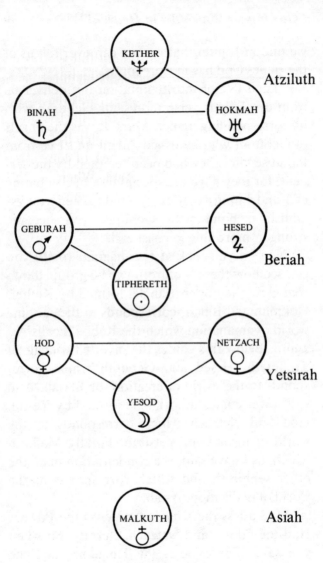

The Tree of Life

bond between yourself and the last sephiroth of the Tree of Life.

Are you beginning, now, to have some inkling of the vast scope of this short and apparently simple prayer Jesus gave us? It contains the whole universe. What immense vistas it opens before our eyes! And what I have told you today is only a fraction of all its wonder. If you think about it and meditate on it you will discover a great many more for yourself.

May light and peace be with you!

# 2

# "MY FATHER AND I ARE ONE"

If you study the history of religions you will see that when Moses proclaimed that Yahveh was the only true God he was saying something absolutely revolutionary. But the God of Moses struck terror into the hearts of men. He was a stern implacable deity, a devouring fire; before him men were fearful, trembling creatures, living under the permanent threat of annihilation if they failed to keep his commandments. And then came Jesus who proclaimed that God was our Father and that we were His Children. The great gulf between ourselves and God became less. Men even discovered that they had family ties with God and this changed everything. But in fact where did the change lie? In ourselves, in our heads and hearts: it came home to men that they were closer to God. They could feel this closeness.

And now, the time has come to go a step further. As long as you imagine God to be some-

where out there, in a part of the universe called
Heaven, surrounded by His angels and archangels, you have a purely objective view of Him.
You feel that He is outside you. Even if He is
your Father and you His son, He is still on the
outside. Of course, God may well exist, objec-
tively, outside man but the trouble is that if man
perceives God as exterior to himself, he becomes
too conscious of his own limitations, too aware
of the barriers between himself and God: too
many worlds, too many stars, the infinite
reaches of space, lie between God and man,
making it impossible to come close to Him.

If we think of God as being totally separate
from us then we too must necessarily be separate
from Him and we are bound to feel that we share
the fate of mere objects. But what exactly is an
"object"? Well, take a farmer, for example, or a
craftsman or labourer: he uses tools, objects
which are totally distinct from himself. He may
use them for a while and then lay them aside until he needs them again. And this is the impression we have if we believe that we exist outside
God: God can pick us up or leave us where we
are, like any other object. Look at a potter with
his pots or a housewife with her saucepans: if
the saucepans were conscious wouldn't they
groan and grumble if their owner left them on
the shelf for too long? "When she used us," they

would say, "at least we were warm and we loved the noise the spoon made as it scraped us. But that is all over now, she's forgotten all about us: she's so heartless and wicked!"

What do you expect? If we are like pots or pans in relation to God it is only normal if He forgets us from time to time. We cannot blame Him for that. What would you think if one of your saucepans dared to come and accuse you of abandoning it? You are mistress in your own kitchen and you do what you like. Then why do we rebel and blame God when we feel abandoned? It is neither logical nor just. The day you live in Him, in His head or His hand then, yes, you will be with Him at every moment, but otherwise you must expect to feel left out from time to time.

Believe me, present-day philosophical and religious conceptions will soon have to change. At the moment people still think it is normal to keep God at a distance. They are all convinced that that is how it should be. But then why do they raise an outcry when they suffer the consequences of their attitude?

As I have already told you, one day there will be a third testament to complete the teaching of the two existing testaments and it will emphasize and insist on this essential truth: man must learn to come closer to God and to feel that He is truly within him. When he does he will never again have the impression that God has abandoned him.

In point of fact, we are forced to admit that if we feel abandoned by God it is because we have abandoned Him. Are we always close to Him? On our First Communion day, perhaps, we prayed and felt His presence for a few minutes but since then, for the next forty or fifty years, have we ever really thought of Him? And if not, why should He think of us? What are we? Do we think we are so important to God that He should constantly be attentive to us?

Of course, I do not deny that we are, perpetually, in God's mind, but very differently from the way we imagine! When a baby is born Cosmic Intelligence gives it all it needs for its life on earth, nothing is missing: head, arms and legs, all the organs... it is all there. Babies are sent to earth fully equipped like soldiers going into battle: they get guns, boots, a helmet, ammunition... and then they have to fend for themselves. And we, too, have all we need: life, health, strength, intelligence... the Lord has given us all that, plus all we need to keep them in good condition and we only have ourselves to blame if we don't know how to use them correctly.

In the past, people were taught to keep their distance from God and many still think that this is a more respectful attitude. But truth has thousands upon thousands of facets and the time is ripe, now, to go a step further. We have to realize that God is here, inside us, and that we are a part, an infinitely small part of Him. He is the Whole and we are minute particles of that Whole. If the God to whom you pray is somewhere, out in space, beyond the stars, how can your prayers ever reach Him? Oh, I know, I once said that prayer can reach into the four corners of the universe, but it takes so long for it to travel through infinite space! And all the time the Lord is right there, close to you, within you. All you have to do is to pick up the phone and say: "Hello, God..." and you will be put through at once. Don't be shocked. I am not being disrespectful. It is just a manner of speaking.

So now, when you meditate, try to practice this. If you can get used to feeling that God is within you it will not be long before you begin to feel the effects. You will not have the feeling of being abandoned nearly so often. At the moment you alternate between periods of happiness and periods of gloom. At one moment you experience joy, inspiration and rapture, and then, all of a sudden, you find yourself in the desert and all is parched and arid. It is then that you think God has abandoned you.

Let me draw a comparison: it is a lovely day,

the sun is shining, but clouds are beginning to gather, they soon hide the sun and there is nothing you can do about it. You would like to go on enjoying the light and warmth of the sun's rays, but it is no longer possible. So what can you do? You will simply have to wait, and while you are waiting you will have the impression that the sun has abandoned you. But of course it has not really abandoned you. It is just that you are too far away, you are under a layer of cloud. But if you take a plane, or a balloon, and go up above the clouds, then nothing can come between you and the sun. It is still there, it never stops shining, it had not abandoned you therefore; all it means is that you had lost altitude, you had dropped down below the cloud cover. If someone is always joyful and inspired, it is a sure sign that he has risen above the clouds: the sun is always shining for him. He basks permanently in its light and warmth.... The explanation is really very simple, isn't it?

Now, since that feeling of loneliness and abandonment comes from ourselves, why not change something in our own attitude? What is the point of staying below the layer of cloud that is preventing us from receiving the joys and revelations the sun is ready to give us?

Well, here you have the whole point of Initiation: Initiation teaches us how to rise so far above the clouds that we no longer depend on anything or anyone else, that we become invulnerable, unassailable, invincible and immortal! Yes, there is no other way: we must continually rise to ever greater heights. Even our notion of God needs to rise, to come closer to Him, so close that we begin to find God within, so intimately, so deeply within us that we bathe continually in His presence.

I know that it is not easy to conceive of God as inseparable from ourselves. But I can give you some exercises which will help. A disciple of an initiatic Teaching knows that within him dwells a cosmic Being of which he is only dimly aware and that he has to uproot his consciousness from the narrow confines of his own lower nature so that it can melt into that boundless consciousness within him. This Being, this spark of Divinity lives in him and it is his task to seek until he finds it.

You must understand that there are two poles: the "you" that is here and now, with your awareness of yourself, in other words, your lower self; and then there is your higher, sublime Self of which you are not yet fully aware. But that Self does exist, he lives and is at work within you. You do not yet know just what he is doing but it is possible for you to picture him in your imagination. From your own lower level

you can imagine the glorious Being dwelling
within you who is seeking to manifest himself
through you, who is seeking to recognize his
own features shining through the gross, unsubtle
material that you are. He knows himself on high
but he wants, now, to know himself through the
medium of the opaque matter of which you are
made. If you continue to use your imagination
in this way so as to come ever closer to your
Higher Self, this practice will one day generate
such light within you that your consciousness
will be released from its present bonds. You will
dwell in such light, such radiant splendour that
you will feel yourself really and truly one with
that sublime Being, your higher Self.

I am not saying that this is easy, of course;
but it is one of the most powerful and effective
exercises you can do. If you can get into the habit of doing it from time to time your efforts will
be richly rewarded. And then, whatever you
may be doing, your superconsciousness will always be there with you, because you will have
established a bond between you. As long as you
remain on the outside of God you are depriving
yourself of His gifts, He cannot give them to you
because you and He belong to two different
worlds, cut off from each other because you are
tuned to different wavelengths. But if you learn
to tune in there will no longer be that great gap

between you and God, you will begin to feel that
you are someone else, you are God Himself who
is manifesting Himself in you. This is what Jesus
meant when he said, "My Father and I are one."

Of course, it is not given to everyone to rise
to such heights. The laws of destiny determine
whether or not we shall do so in our present incarnation. But if you make the effort you will at
least rise above certain limitations. Human beings do not know how to make use of the means
God makes available to them. He has given us
the possibility of becoming like Him. All men
have that possibility and it is only because of
what they are at the moment that they do not
use it. They know nothing about it, they feel
nothing of it, most of them remain permanently
on a lower level. And yet no one is completely
tied to his lower self, even those with the most
meagre resources are capable of surpassing
themselves, and if they tuned in mentally and
sought to discover those regions where God
dwells they would realize this. But... how many
will ever attempt to change something in themselves? Of course, as I have already said, the reason is very simple : it all depends on where they
put their priorities. If all they really care about is
money and pleasure, if spirituality does not
enter into their scheme of things, how can you
expect them to make any progress? But if you

find someone who gives priority to light, love and beauty, who places the spirit before all else and does not spend his time worrying about whether he is going to be rich or poor, whether he is going to eat or go hungry, whether he will be well-dressed or in rags and whether he will be respected or ridiculed... for a man such as this, everything is possible.

# 3

# "BE YE PERFECT,
# EVEN AS YOUR FATHER WHO IS
# IN HEAVEN IS PERFECT"

# I

Modern man is in the grip of the worst possible form of slavery: the loss of that light which flowed from all the sanctuaries of Antiquity to teach men that they were sons of God. When Jesus came and revealed this tremendous truth to the multitudes he was crucified; it had always been concealed from the masses up to then, for fear that once they realized their own dignity they would no longer submit to the rules and regulations imposed by the Sadducees and Pharisees. Jesus Christ was the most revolutionary of all God's messengers. He flouted all the old laws and was made to pay on the cross for his boldness in telling the people they were all children of the same Father.

The Old Testament had already declared: "Ye are gods", but this had been deliberately ignored, and still is, to this day. And yet the key to men's salvation is in their recognition of the fact that they are all children of the same Father:

God, and of the same Mother: Nature or the Universal Soul. Until they realize this they will never know their true nature, they will be out of touch with the essential core of their own reality and, naturally, they will continue to suffer. Whether they refuse to acknowledge the divine origin of mankind or whether they simply neglect to seek out the divine spark within themselves, they will all suffer, for it is impossible to find happiness if one rejects the basic reality of man's divine essence.

Yes, God has planted in the heart of man a spark, a seed, a model of perfection and splendour and has enjoined him to correspond more and more closely to that model until he becomes one with it. This was what Jesus was saying when he told his disciples "Be ye perfect as your Father who is in heaven is perfect." But how can we be as perfect as our Heavenly Father if we have never seen Him and do not know what He is like? In fact, it is not necessary to see Him. In every one of us slumbers, like a seed, that image of our Heavenly Father's perfection, so all we need to do is nourish and water that seed and breathe life into it and, gradually, we shall come closer and closer to perfection. Deep in each man's heart lies this seed engraved with the indestructible image of divine perfection, but it needs something to nourish and strengthen it, something to stimulate its growth and that something is a high ideal: a lofty ideal is the essential catalyst if that seed is to grow into a healthy plant. It is because of this that one can say that man comes into the world with a mission... but be sure you understand the term "mission" correctly. A great many, very ordinary people delude themselves with the idea that they have a mission: they have no special gifts or talents but they have got it in their heads that they have been sent by Heaven to put the world to rights... and when one sees how puny and powerless they are one can only be amazed! Of course we do have a mission, all of us, but we must be sure we know what it is. Our mission is to bring all the talents and virtues Heaven has sown in us to their full flowering. It is perfectly possible that, from time to time, Heaven should choose a very special being for a very special mission, but the mission of all men is to grow and develop until they reach perfection. Even if their talents are not outstanding, even if they seem not much better than animals, this is their mission: to improve themselves and work at their own evolution. Unfortunately there are always plenty of "takers" for false missions – people who think that, like Joan of Arc, they are going to save France – but their veritable mission does not interest them and that is a pity. First and foremost we must fulfil the mission God has entrusted to each one of us: to become perfect as He is perfect. And if we cannot complete our task in one short incarnation, we shall come back and go on with it in another. For when Jesus told us to be as perfect as our Heavenly Father, reincarnation was obviously implicit in the command. Otherwise, how could he, who was so wise and enlightened, possibly have asked human beings to become perfect in only one life. Is it possible that he did not fully realize the weakness of men or the immense majesty of God? No, if he had not counted with reincarnation this precept would have been nonsense, whereas in the light of reincarnation it makes perfect sense. And if Jesus demanded perfection of us it is because he knew that perfection was the law of the entire universe.

God is perfect and man is not. But man can become perfect, for the Book of Genesis tells us that man was created in the image of God: "And God said, let us make man in our image, after our likeness: and let them have dominion over the fish of the sea, and over the fowl of the air and over the cattle...." And a few lines further on, it says, "So God created man in His own image, in the image of God created He him." The word "image" is repeated in this second verse, but not the word "likeness"... and

one may ask, "Why?" and "What is the difference between image and likeness?" It means
that God intended to create man in His own
image and likeness but He did not do so. He
created him only in His image, in other words
He gave man all the faculties He himself possesses but He did not give him the full fruition of
those faculties: the likeness.

It might help us to understand better if we
take the example of an acorn: this tiny nut is in
the image of its parent, the oak-tree, by which I
mean that it possesses potentially all the oak's
characteristics and qualities but it does not seem
to be in the least like its parent-tree. Just look at
the difference between them! The acorn can
only become an oak if it is planted. Man is in the
image of God, which means that he possesses
the same attributes: wisdom, love, power and so
on, but to an infinitely lesser degree. When, in
the course of time, he attains his full stature he
will be like God because he will possess the divine attributes in all their fullness.

So you see that the evolutionary process, the
passage from "image" to "likeness" implies
reincarnation. God said, "Let us make man in
our image, after our likeness" but He did not
bring the likeness to completion. "God created
man in His own image, in the image of God
created He him." By leaving out the word "like-

ness" and repeating the word "image" Moses secretly implied the idea of reincarnation.

"But," you will object, "there's no mention of reincarnation in the Gospels." Well, that is where you are mistaken. True, the word is not mentioned explicitly, but it is there, as plain as day, for anyone who can read.

Let's have a look at some of the questions Jesus or his disciples asked, and the answers they received. One day Jesus asked, "Whom do men say that I am?" and we may well wonder what this question really means. Have you often heard people asking a question like that? And now, look at the answer he got from his disciples: "Some say that thou art John the Baptist; some, Elias; and others, Jeremias, or one of the prophets." How can you say that someone is quite another person especially if that other person has been dead for a long time... unless, of course, you believe in reincarnation?

On another occasion Jesus and his disciples met a man who was born blind, and his disciples asked, "Master, who did sin, this man, or his parents, that he was born blind?" How could this man possibly have sinned in his mother's womb before he was born? No, either the question makes no sense or we have to admit that Jesus and his disciples took it for granted that the blind man had lived on earth before. The

disciples asked if it was his parents who had
sinned because they knew from Jewish law that
although every misfortune or infirmity is a result
of having broken the law it does not necessarily
mean that the one who pays the debt is the one
who sinned, for it quite often happens that
someone is allowed to sacrifice himself for another.

This was a generally accepted belief amongst
the Jews of that time and the disciples' question,
therefore, implied that they knew the blind man
was paying a debt incurred through a breach of
the law, for no man is born blind by chance or
because it had pleased God to afflict him in that
way – as Christians imagine! And Jesus answered, "Neither hath this man sinned, nor his
parents: but that the works of God should be
manifest in him." In other words the man was
blind so that, passing this way, I should heal him
and the people should come to believe in me."
Men suffer for two reasons, either because they
have sinned and have to be punished or because,
being sinless themselves, they take on someone
else's karma and sacrifice themselves in order to
hasten their own evolution. But there is also a
third category: those who have completed their
evolution and are completely free; they have no
need to return to earth. And yet, very often, they
do so because they are willing to suffer every

imaginable disease, pain or infirmity, even mar-
tyrdom, in order to help other human beings.
That blind man comes into this third category.

And if you are still not convinced, here are
some other arguments. One day Jesus was told
that John the Baptist had been put in prison and
the Gospel story simply says: "Now when Jesus
had heard that John was cast into prison, he de-
parted into Galilee." Shortly after that, Herod
ordered the execution of John the Baptist and
his head was cut off. After the Transfiguration
the disciples asked Jesus, "Why then do the
scribes say that Elias must first come?" Jesus
answered: "Elias truly shall first come, and restore all things. But I say unto you, that Elias is
come already, and they knew him not, but they
have done unto him whatsoever they listed."
And the Gospel adds: "Then the disciples understood that he spoke unto them of John the
Baptist." It is obvious, therefore, that John the
Baptist was the reincarnation of Elias. But there
is another text, too, which tells us the same
thing: when an angel appeared to Zacharias to
tell him that his wife, Elizabeth, would bear a
son, he said: "And he shall go before God in the
spirit and power of Elias."

Now, let's look at the story of Elias and see
what he had done to deserve being beheaded
when he came back as John the Baptist. It is a

very interesting story. Elias lived at the time of
King Ahab whose Queen, Jezebel, was the
daughter of the King of Sidon and, because of
Jezebel, Ahab and his people worshipped Baal.
One day Elias came before King Ahab and reproached him for being unfaithful to the God of
Israel, saying: "There shall not be dew nor rain
these years, but according to my word." Then,
instructed by God, Elias went and hid in the
mountains so that the King could not find him.
At the end of three years the country was ra-
vaged by drought, the people were starving and
God sent Elias to King Ahab once again. When
Ahab saw Elias he reproached him bitterly for
having caused the drought, but Elias replied: "I
have not troubled Israel; but thou, and thy father's house, in that ye have forsaken the commandments of the Lord, and thou hast followed
Baal.... Now therefore send, and gather to me all
Israel unto Mount Carmel, and the prophets of
Baal... four hundred and fifty." When they were
all assembled, Elias told them they would now
see who was the real God. "I, even I only, remain a Prophet of the Lord, but Baal's prophets
are four hundred and fifty men. Let them give us
two bullocks and let them choose one bullock
for themselves and cut it in pieces and lay it on
wood, and put no fire under; and I will dress the
other bullock and lay it on wood and put no fire

under. And call ye on the name of your gods, and I will call on the name of the Lord, and the god that answereth by fire, let him be God."

The prophets did as he said and all morning long they invoked the name of Baal, "O Baal, hear us!" But there was no voice, nor any that answered... and Elias mocked them and said, "Cry aloud: for he is a god; either he is talking or he is pursuing, or he is in a journey, or per adventure he sleepeth and must be awaked!" The prophets cried all the louder and even slashed their own bodies with knives, for, being magicians, they hoped that the blood would attract ghosts and spectres who would set fire to their offering. But nothing happened. So when evening came and there was still no answer from Baal, Elias decided that was enough, and taking twelve stones he built an altar with a trench all around. Then he put wood on the altar, cut the bullock in pieces and laid the pieces on the wood and poured water all over the altar and the sacrificial bullock until it filled the trench. When everything was ready Elias called on God: "Lord God of Abraham, Isaac, and of Israel, let it be known this day that thou art God in Israel, and that I am thy servant, and that I have done all these things at thy word." Then the fire of the Lord fell from Heaven with such power that everything was consumed: nothing was left, neither victim, nor wood, nor stones, nor water and the terrified people recognized that the God of Elias was the true God. But Elias, who was no doubt a little too pleased with himself, ordered that the four hundred and fifty priests be taken down to a nearby brook and massacred.

This is why, as was to be expected, he too had his throat cut. For there is a law which Jesus referred to in the Garden of Gethsemane when Peter lunged at the high priest's servant and cut off his ear. He said: "Put up again thy sword into its place: for all they that take the sword shall perish with the sword." Now the truth of these words is not always demonstrated in the space of one lifetime. Elias, for instance, did not die by the sword. Not only was he not massacred but a fiery chariot was sent to take him straight to Heaven. It was only later, when he returned to earth as John the Baptist that he received his punishment. Jesus knew who he was and did nothing to save him: justice had to follow its course.

The Christians believed in reincarnation until the fourth century, as did the Jews, Egyptians, Indians, Tibetans, etc.... But no doubt the Church Fathers said to themselves that this belief gave people too much time, they were improving too slowly, and if the idea of reincarnation was eliminated they would improve more

quickly, they would have only one life in which
to become perfect! Gradually the Church in-
vented more and more dreadful things to fright-
en people into obedience; by the Middle Ages,
all they believed in was devils, Hell, and everlasting damnation. The Church abolished belief
in reincarnation, therefore, so that people would
be forced to improve through fear and dread, but
not only did they not improve, they became
worse... and ignorant to boot! And this is why
we must recover this belief, for without it nothing is true, nothing in life makes sense and the
God whom Jesus presented as our Father, is
made to seem a monster of cruelty.

If you need further proof, go and ask a priest
or a pastor why such and such a person is rich,
good-looking, intelligent and healthy; why he
succeeds in everything he does, whereas another
is poor, ugly, sickly, plagued with bad luck and a
lack of brains. He will reply that it is the will of
God. Perhaps he will speak of predestination
and grace, but you will not be any the wiser for
it. Either way it is God's will.

If this answer is true we can only conclude
that God is so capricious that He does whatever
He fancies, that He gives everything to some and
nothing to others. Well, for the sake of argument, let's accept that that is so: after all God is
God and if it is His will, all we can do is bow our

heads and accept it. But in that case how can you possibly explain why He should then be furious and outraged if people who have never had a chance to learn any better behave badly or become atheistic, unscrupulous and vicious. If it is really He who has given them that mentality, and sent them into the world with so little intelligence and such evil in their hearts, why should He then punish them? He is all-powerful. Couldn't He have made them kind, honest, intelligent and wise? Not only is it supposed to be His fault if they commit crimes but in addition He punishes them for their crimes! Something is very wrong here! Why is God not more consistent, more logical and just? He could at least leave people alone. But no... He has to torment them in Hell for all Eternity!

And there, again, something is terribly wrong. How long have they been sinning for? Thirty, forty, maybe fifty years? Well, all right, let them stay in Hell for the same number of years, but no more. Not forever... that would be unbelievably cruel!

Whereas if we accept the truth of reincarnation everything looks quite different: God is really and truly Master of the universe, the noblest, most sublime and most just and we can understand that if we are poor, unintelligent and unhappy it is our own fault because we have not made good use of all the wealth He gave us at the beginning. We wanted to try all kinds of costly experiments and He is so immensely generous and tolerant that He let us misuse our freedom. No doubt He said to Himself, "Oh, well! They'll suffer when they come a cropper but it doesn't matter. I'll still shower them with my wealth and my love. They have a lot of reincarnations ahead of them. They are my children and sooner or later they'll come back to me."

So now you can see more clearly what Jesus' words mean: "Be ye perfect even as your Father who is in Heaven is perfect." This precept has been rejected as being too difficult to fulfil, whereas, in fact, the point is not so much whether you are going to succeed or fail in it, but to take it seriously as an ideal to be aimed for. Shall we achieve our ideal? And if so, when? That does not depend on us and we should not even bother our heads about it. Perhaps no human being has ever achieved it; divine perfection is so infinitely beyond us. But we must still desire and long for it, for it is this aspiration which sparks the qualities and virtues dormant in us into life, which makes it possible for us to benefit from their existence. It is this aspiration which sets them in motion so that we can actually feel their help and support. The Creator has planted untold possibilities in men, but a high ideal is the fuse which is needed to make them active and effective. A high ideal is what sets everything in motion.

## II

A seed is a living organism which survives and fulfils its own particular function thanks to the fact that it constantly draws on and nourishes itself with the forces and materials available in the cosmos around it. And the function or mission of a seed is to resemble the tree from which it came. The Creator has given to every seed this vocation: to become like its father, the tree. So, unless it has some inherent defect, once it is sown, all of its activity is directed towards the fulfilment of its vocation and for this it chooses from amongst the elements around it, taking only those which suit it and leaving the others. In this way it is able to express every detail of the blueprint within it. And this is exactly what happens with man. Since God created man in His image, he is capable, if he develops as he should, of becoming like his Heavenly Father.

What is there in a seed? If you open it up and

look at it under a microscope you will not see the picture of a tree. And yet, when you plant it, that insignificant little grain will gradually produce a magnificent plant: roots and stem, leaves, flowers and fruits. Obviously, under the microscope you cannot see plans of branches and leaves and so on because they are etheric. If you were able to see what exists on the etheric plane that would be different. Then you would see the blueprint for the whole tree that will spring, one day, from that seed.

Growth is something that follows a plan, and unfolds along predetermined lines of force so that a plant always grows up with exactly the same characteristics as its parent-plant: shape, size, colour, taste, scent and any special properties. Everybody finds this so normal and natural that no one ever stops to wonder about it and yet if you think about this, it seems a perpetual miracle! But what is truly extraordinary is that the growing process of a seed can reveal the mystery of man. For man, too, has an inner blueprint which determines and directs all his inherent forces and energies. What is this blueprint and how can it be put into actual practice? That is what I want to talk to you about now.

Every building has to have an initial plan, prepared by a designer, the architect. Workmen are needed to put up the building, and then, of course, there have to be building materials as well. This is equally true for a child in its mother's womb: it is formed according to the blueprint or programme drawn up by the Lords of Destiny, a plan which takes account of everything that person has acquired or merited in the course of previous lives. The body built by the baby's mother is its house, its dwelling place and it, too, is constructed according to the blueprint. When a human being comes into this world, therefore, the lines of force along which his destiny will unfold are already inscribed as in a germ within him, just like the genetic programme contained in the seed of a plant, and the child grows up to conform to that image.

In point of fact a human being does not take shape and develop from only one germ, but from seven. The seven germs correspond to man's seven bodies: atmic, buddhic, causal, mental, astral, etheric and physical, which support the different facets of his life: physical (the physical body), emotional (the astral body), intellectual (the mental body) and spiritual (the causal, buddhic and atmic bodies). During man's descent through the different layers and spheres of space, he receives seven germs destined to grow into his seven bodies, starting with the subtlest, the atmic body, and ending with the most densely material, the physical body.

But let's get back to the seed. People who have travelled in India have told of watching a fakir plant a mango seed, for instance, and after only a very short time, when it had grown into a bush, distribute its fruit to the onlookers. The explanation for this phenomenon is that the fakir works with a substance which Indians call Akâsha. Akâsha is an etheric substance present in the atmosphere, which can be used to accelerate the growth of plants and make fruit ripen very rapidly. Someone who knows how to concentrate on akâshic energy can make a tree, which would normally take months and years to grow, reach maturity in only a few hours.

But, although a great many people have studied this phenomenon (not to mention all those who are convinced that it is all a hoax), no one has ever discovered that a human being can hasten his own growth toward perfection in the same way. It is man's vocation to reach the perfection of his Heavenly Father. Even if it takes hundreds and thousands of years, man will eventually attain divine perfection, for it is built into him. But what no one realizes is that it does not have to take thousands of years: it can be achieved in the space of only one incarnation. Yes, it can be done, but only if someone is capable of bringing to light the image of God concealed within him and of nursing and nourishing

it with that akâshic substance, the cosmic elec-
tricity which the Emerald Tablet of Hermes
Trismegistus calls Telesma. Whatever one calls
it, it is that primordial force, "the strong fortitude of all strength" as Hermes Trismegistus
called it. It is this force that comes from the sun,
of which the sun is the distributor and the inexhaustible fountainhead. One of the manifesta-
tions of that force is love, the love that makes
worlds go round, the love of which sexual love is
only one limited aspect.

So, there you have it, the rare, almost unknown science of how to use that energy to reach
the divine perfection etched into the seed within
us, just as the genetic programme of a plant is
etched into each seed. The seed does not look in
the least like a tree, but it bears the image of a
tree in its structure. Given favourable conditions
it will grow into a tree because, before ever it attains physical maturity, the full-grown tree exists on a subtler level. So we who are seeds can
take a lesson from this: our vocation is to grow
into the likeness of our Heavenly Father by ad-
hering more and more closely to His image within, by fine-tuning ourselves to His wavelength
and learning to vibrate in rhythm with Him.

But we can also think of the divine image
within us as our Higher Self, the Self we strive to

become, the Self with whom we endeavour to identify, just as a dull, black, insignificant little seed identifies with and becomes a giant of the forest.

Look at an oak-tree: it started life as a miserable little acorn, just fit to be gobbled up by a pig. And then, a few years later what do we see but a magnificent tree, the pride of the forest! Its leaves purify the air, birds build their nests in its branches, children hang their swings from it, hikers stop to rest in its shade, artists are inspired to paint it, country folk collect firewood. An oak-tree... what a noble and inspiring sight. And who could have guessed what that acorn, that little bit of nothing would turn into? And we too are little bits of nothing, but if we know how to use that "strong fortitude of all strength" to work at becoming the divine image within, we too shall become what the Lord intended us to be.

The Bible says that God created man in His image and likeness. The image is in us. God Himself put it there and now it is up to us to do all in our power to reach the likeness. The only human activity worthy of the name is to work at becoming like our Heavenly Father, to make every possible effort to reach that goal, to go just a little bit further, a little bit higher every day in

order to see things differently in their true
beauty, their true grandeur.

Yes, God created man in His image and that
image is to be found in the germ of our atmic
body. God's image could not be on the physical,
astral or mental levels, on those levels its manifestation would be totally inadequate; the results would be too weak and inept. It is on the
higher level, in our spirit, on the level of absolute beauty and perfection that we are moulded
after the image of God. If this perfection is still
invisible it is because our other, grosser bodies
are like thick, opaque layers of skin which hide
it from view. But he who knows how to focus all
his powers of concentration on the sublime germ
of absolute light and love within, will gradually
make it grow and blossom.

If, on the other hand, someone neglects to
nourish and vivify the divine seed within, with
pure, noble thoughts and feelings, it will remain
infertile, and he will continue to live his me-
diocre life unaware that it is within his power to
transform it. But once a disciple is capable of fo-
cusing his powers of thought and love on that
germ, not only does it begin to thrive and blossom, but its influence spreads to his other bodies
and, within the much narrower limits of their
possibilities, they too begin a process of transformation. Once he has begun to activate that inner

image it gradually influences all the cells of his body and creates a marvellous state of harmony throughout.

The Kabbala teaches that the first man who lived in the Garden of Eden, the Cosmic man who is known as Adam Kadmon, had exactly the same countenance as the Lord. But later, when his intellect developed (this process is symbolized by the serpent coiled round the Tree of the Knowledge of Good and Evil), he was tempted to broaden his sphere of knowledge and left Paradise. In other words he descended into the ever denser layers of material creation, where he experienced cold, darkness, disease and death. At that time the spirits of Nature and the animals ceased to serve and obey him as before and began to torment him.

When man's countenance is restored to its original beauty all the spirits of the universe will obey him once again and will give him all that his heart desires. But until then he will be like the Prodigal Son who, having left his father's house to enjoy life in his own way, ended up herding pigs. At least the Prodigal Son finally understood that he would do better to go back to his father's house.... What about you? Will you end by understanding that you must go back to the Source in order to be in possession, once again, of your Heavenly Father's light, love and life?

Go back to the Source... that is what we do every morning when we go and watch the sun rising, for the sun represents that Source, the Godhead, to us, here, on earth. No Initiate would ever say that the sun was God, and that is not what I am saying, either. But seen as light, warmth and life, the sun is the most admirable symbol of the Blessed Trinity. If we put ourselves in its presence, consciously, every morning, it will nourish and strengthen our own little trinity: the intellect which is groping for the light, the heart which hungers for warmth and the will which seeks life and energy. Christians refuse to regard the sun as an expression of the Trinity. They seem to think it is a primitive, pagan notion, but their own symbols are totally ineffectual because there is no life in them; they express nothing, they radiate nothing.

By contemplating the sun you are opening all your doors to that Akâshic energy, Telesma, which flows in such abundance from the sun and fills all of space. You are making it possible for that force to enter into you and fertilize the divine seed, God's image, lying dormant in the innermost core of your being. And as soon as the divine image within is revealed in all its splendour, the forces and spirits of Nature, the four Elements, will hasten to serve you. If you ask them for something it will be their joy to give it to you, because they respect the image they see in you. But if they cannot recognize the divine image in you, they will resist and even destroy you. This is why, when someone practices black magic and attempts to command the spirits of Nature, they turn on him and tear him to pieces. They refuse to obey someone in whom they see no love, light or purity and if he tries to force them to do his will with magic spells they simply take their revenge. The only power they respect is the power of light radiating from an Initiate in whom they recognize the authentic likeness of God.

Why are Christians left to grope in the dark with such ineffectual, useless, even harmful notions? Two thousand years ago Jesus said, "Be ye perfect even as your Father who is in heaven is perfect": do you see Christians really and truly seeking to attain to the perfection of our Heavenly Father? They are still puny, wretched, jealous and vindictive, full of anger and sensuality.... Is that a reflection of what God is like? The information and understanding they have been given have been inadequate to enable them to transform themselves. They need something more. Some of you may say, "But what more could they have? They have it all. It's all there, in the Gospels." Yes, I know. The only question is: have they understood the Gospels? I am perhaps more convinced than any of you that the Gospels contain great treasures, but many of these treasures have not yet been disclosed, still less put into practice. Yes, the Gospels contain it all, but not much of it has penetrated into the heads of Christians!

Christ's philosophy leads men toward the attainment of the highest of all ideals, that of resembling the divine model secreted in his atmic body. If Jesus could say, "Be ye perfect as your Father who is in heaven is perfect", it was because the image of the Father's perfection lies dormant in every human creature and if he cares for it, if he nourishes and vivifies it, he will gradually grow into that perfection. But only the high ideal can help him reach that goal.

A woman who is expecting a baby does not know how it is being formed, she has no conscious control over the complex processes taking place in her body, and yet the baby is formed and the formative process obeys every detail of the instructions contained in the seed that fertilized her. She is unaware of how all this is taking place, but in her subconscious are forces which know exactly what to do. And, in the same way, each one of you can watch over the growth and development of the divine seed within you. When you pray or meditate, therefore, try to rise to the highest point of your being, for it is there, at the peak – or, if you prefer, at the heart – of your being (the expression is different, but the inner movement is the same), that you will find the Source. And here, in this Source, waiting to be released, are all the forces and energies you need to transform you, to change everything in you down to the least cell, the very vibrations of the tiniest atom of your body.

# 4

# "SEEK YE FIRST THE KINGDOM OF GOD AND HIS JUSTICE"

If you experiment with a variety of activities in life and make a sincere analysis of your own reactions, you will come to realize that no activity on earth can compare to that which Jesus recommended: "Seek ye first the Kingdom of God and His justice and all these things shall be added unto you." No other activity is so useful, so beautiful, so glorious! "The Kingdom of God" contains and includes everything, all the most precious qualities and virtues: wisdom, love, strength, beauty and harmony... above all: harmony. In other words, if your life conforms to this principle it will be a beneficial influence in the world.

You may wonder why Jesus said: The Kingdom of God and His justice." Why "justice"? It seems obvious that God's Kingdom has no need of justice. If it needed justice surely it would not be the Kingdom of God, for God's Kingdom is the Kingdom of love, generosity and bounteousness. Yes, but justice is necessary in the physical

world in which we live, so when God's Kingdom
comes down to earth it does need justice.

In Heaven no one commits crimes so there is
no need for justice. Those who dwell in Heaven
are overflowing with light and love. Justice is
needed only when someone breaks the law. So
this is why we speak of the Kingdom of God and
His justice, because, when the Kingdom of God
is established on earth there will be some who
are still not sufficiently enlightened to be ruled
only by the law of love. Even then, not all human beings will be instantly transformed: only
an elite. The wisest and best amongst men will
establish the Kingdom of God and the masses
will accept their authority. There will have to be
justice; it is not possible to have a land without
laws. But the laws will be there not only to punish and restrain wrongdoers, but also to give
guidance and direction to all.

So it is no use expecting people to become
perfect overnight, even when the Kingdom of
God is established on this earth. It won't happen! It is a process that takes time. To begin
with there will be a minority of very advanced
people who understand and accept all that the
Kingdom of God involves, and it is they who
will rule. The others will just have to follow, as
the tail has to follow the head. They will have
the opportunity to join with the minority that

constitutes the Kingdom of God and when they see the new life that is open to them and a new social organization, so tremendously beneficial for all, no one will object. When this day comes we shall no longer see what we see now: each country trying to organize everything for its own benefit and trying to expand its sphere of influence abroad to the detriment of others, because each one has the ambition to be the first, the greatest, the most powerful.

The Kingdom of God is a world of harmony, joy and happiness and such a world could not survive on this earth without justice, for even when the Heavenly Kingdom is established not everybody will be capable of appreciating this superabundance of divine grace and of using it only for good. So it will be necessary to impose justice, but a new, different justice, not that imposed by the ignorant who often make useless, unjust laws.

"Seek ye the Kingdom of God and His justice", and not your own, for your own, personal justice is too often based on self-interest. Certainly, everyone has to have a roof over his head. Everyone needs food and clothing, but if you are not interested in anything beyond this, if you restrict yourself to these concerns... well, this is what robs you of your joy and enthusiasm.

Why? Because all these things which preoccupy you day and night are incapable of triggering the sublime forces slumbering within you. One day, in the future, the effects of various human occupations will be studied in laboratories and it will be found that people's general well-being is determined by their preoccupations: what they are interested in, what they think about and the area or circle in which their preoccupations confine them. Science will give us proof of this one day, but I am not waiting for science to pronounce judgment before I believe it and act upon it.

So, now that you know this you can put the knowledge to use and decide to change your point of view, to broaden your mental attitudes and the way you function. If you do so you will soon see that, while everyone around you seems to be sunk in their own wretchedness, you are like a fish in water or a bird in the air; you shine... and all your problems are resolved with ease. All this you gain simply by living on a different level, which is just as real, in fact far more real, than all the rest.

What counts most is the way in which you spend your energies: how do you use them and to what end? If you are depressed and unhappy it is because you move in too narrow a circle. Expand your sphere of interest and you will attract forces and living entities to instruct and

help you. This is the remedy I prescribe for unhappiness: broaden the scope of your mental
activity and if, up to now, you have concentrat-
ed all your attention on your own little family
circle – or even if you are mayor of the village or
President of the Republic – look to wider horizons, infinitely wider horizons. Let your interest
embrace the solar system, the whole cosmos all
the way to its Creator, and you will no longer
feel so small and wretched, so abandoned and
neglected. You will become creative, a positive,
beneficial influence amongst men. The immortal spirits on high will do nothing without calling
on you to take part in their councils to determine the destinies of countries and whole con-
tinents. You don't believe me? You should!
The creatures who dwell in the spheres above
have great respect for human beings who work
with all their heart and soul for the good of mankind. Here, perhaps, you are a nobody: no one
respects you, no one listens to you, but at night,
while you are asleep, divine beings invite you to
take part in their decisions. Here again is something that orthodox science knows nothing
about. It is so far from any true perception of the
mysterious reality of a human being, of the hidden nature of the soul or the spirit and how far-
reaching are their activities.

So, from now on, make up your minds to

break out from the confines of your own petty preoccupations. Understand that there are more things on earth than your wife (or husband), your children, your job and your house! Give priority to the idea of joining forces with the millions and millions of entities in the universe who are working for the coming of the Kingdom. Your lives are worthless if you are not working consciously, and with every means at your disposal, for the sublime ideal of the Kingdom of God. The day you really take this in, seriously, your destiny will change. A new age is upon us, an age in which all men will work for the Kingdom of God because all will realize that they will never achieve their own individual happiness as long as the collective problems of humanity have not found a solution. Some people expect to find happiness by fishing in troubled waters, but they are heading for disappointment! Individuals will find happiness only when the overall situation of the human collectivity has improved, for it is from this collectivity that they draw their strength.

Of course, once you begin working for the coming of the Kingdom, you realize that it is happening neither fast nor easily. And when this first comes home to you, if you are ignorant of initiatic teaching you may feel very disappointed and begin to lose courage. You may have the feeling that all your prayers and hard work are useless. But if you know the laws, even if you do not believe that God's Kingdom will be realized on earth very soon, because of all the wicked, egotistical, ignorant people on earth, you will never cease to long and work for it. And how is it that you will have the courage to keep going? It is because you now know how human beings, and indeed the whole universe, are constructed, and the relationships that bind them each to all. So you know that when your desires and the words and ideas that flow from you are full of light, they trigger forces in the invisible world and these forces are echoed back to you.

Now, I must tell you something that is really extremely important: even if you never actually attain your goal, even if you never manage to establish the Kingdom of God and His justice in the world around you, you must never cease working for it because by doing so you will establish it within yourselves... and it is you who will gain. Believe me, the impersonal, luminous idea of the Kingdom of God is so sublime and contains such power, that it sets in motion untold forces in the depths of the individual. In order to succeed in such a stupendous undertaking as God's Kingdom on earth, a vast network of human beings – millions and millions of people – are going to have to work at it. How could it possibly be otherwise when there are so many, more than four billion people in the world, who oppose it, who have no understanding of it, who listen only to their instincts and lusts?

And then, of course, there are all those learned and intelligent people who say: "But what's the use... it's idiotic to work for something when you know in advance that nothing will ever come of it." Ah, but what they do not know, all those bright people, is that when you work for this exalted cause it is you, yourself, who are the first to benefit from it, because God's Kingdom establishes itself in the hearts of those who love it and long for it, those who seek it. The logic of this is the same as that which governs the law of physics, chemistry and mechanics! The Kingdom of God is a state, a state of harmony, balance, health, joy, happiness, inspiration, poetry... and even if others are unreceptive, at least we can establish it within ourselves. The happiness you wish for others makes you happy, the light you wish to others shines in you, the purity you wish for others purifies you.

Most people are very far from such glorious concerns; they busy themselves with all kinds of little things which are easily achieved, whereas those of you who understand the laws can say to yourselves, "I could easily get all the little things I would like in life. It's not difficult, I could soon wangle it. But then I'd gain neither wisdom, nor happiness, nor fulfilment. I know the law of affinity: if I sow commonplace seed I'll reap a commonplace harvest." Those who do not know this throw themselves into simple, easy, readily attainable undertakings... and that is not intelligent.

Most people are convinced that if only they had such and such a sum of money, or this or that diploma, if they could only afford this trip or marry that woman, they would be content. But it is all an illusion: material achievements or possessions have very little to do with true happiness. One can achieve a great deal outwardly and still be a pauper inwardly. I tell you frankly: I have chosen the most impossible, unattainable goal. I know I shall never manage to make it happen outwardly, but inwardly it is already happening!

You will probably say, "Oh, all that's too bizarre! It's ridiculous. No one else ever gave us such outlandish advice! On the contrary we have always been told we shouldn't fly too high, that it's better to aim for something we can reach easily, something that's within our grasp." Yes, I know. But look around you at the people who have got what they aimed for: are they satisfied? Are they truly happy? For a short while, perhaps. But once they have "arrived" they have no further ambitions and they lose all their enthusiasm and impetus. Whereas others who have never reached their goal are happy because they still have something to look forward to. How can you explain that? The reason is that on the level of human thoughts and aspirations the possibilities are infinite. In the realm of the soul and the spirit man knows no limits. If he feels limited it is because he has imposed limitations on himself. Unfortunately, very few people are capable of persevering in an unattainable dream in the conviction that their own inner life can cause their thoughts and aspirations to be so pure and lustrous that they will carry them to sublime heights. And in those higher realms other, exalted beings and elements which exactly correspond to their own nature and aspirations will be drawn to them.

Even if we cannot establish the Kingdom of God it is still worth working for it, hoping and longing for it, for in that way we do establish it in ourselves and, one day, when a lot of people have restored the Kingdom of peace and harmony within themselves it will inevitably be restored externally on the physical plane also. If men understood their own structure and that of the universe, and if they recognized their own needs, they would say, "I don't care if the Kingdom of God actually gets established on earth or not. All I know is that if I cling to this idea I'll never be bogged down in uncertainty, anxiety and inner chaos again. By thinking of the Kingdom of God I'm working for myself. I'm constantly sending out thoughts charged with light and if no one wants them it doesn't matter. They'll come back to me." This is a reaction that shows true wisdom and understanding.

"Seek ye first the Kingdom of God and His justice and all these things shall be added unto you." Yes, all those who have sincerely sought the Kingdom of God can vouch for it : they have always had all those other things, all they ever needed. As for me, I do not really think those other things are worth bothering about. What do they matter as long as you have the Kingdom of God within? But, just a minute, now : Jesus did not say that you would receive "all these things" when you *possessed* the Kingdom, but when you were still *seeking* it. In other words, even before you possess it, if you seek it and if you hope and long for it with all your heart, so that nothing else can beguile you or lure you away from your ideal, then "all those things" will be given you. But what are "all those things"? I will tell you : they are money, good health, friends, freedom and favourable conditions. Which means that if we seek the Kingdom of God we shall be sure of having whatever we need to enable us to find it.

Once you have the Kingdom it eclipses every
other consideration: it is a state of bliss, harmony, peace, love, purity, perfection and fulfilment. What else could one possibly ask for,
since it includes everything? But until such time
as we actually achieve that "everything" we
need help, we need the means and conditions to
reach our goal... and it is these means and conditions which are "these things" Jesus promised to
those who seek the Kingdom of God.

Now, there is only one thing for you to do
and that is to try to verify the truth of what I am
saying. The trouble is, of course, that the major-
ity of people are tempted by the glitter of so
many other things and those who are really interested in the Kingdom of God are few and far
between. But those who are truly enlightened are
interested only in God's Kingdom and His justice because they know that, in this way, both
heaven and earth will be theirs. Obviously it will
not happen within a few months or even in a few
years, but for those who hunger and thirst only
for what is great and noble nothing is more desirable. Try it! Take the plunge and you will see
for yourselves: all else pales beside this. You
will realize that up to now you had been pursuing shadows, disappointments, emptiness.

I tell you frankly, even if I knew for sure that
the Kingdom of God would never come on earth

I would still go on hoping for it. You see, I realize that it is to my advantage to do so because that state of wholeness and harmony will, at least, come into my own heart and soul and mind. And for you, too: if you understand this law now, today, your life can change at this very instant. You will leave your narrow, workaday preoccupations behind; noble, generous, lofty thoughts and desires will give you wings and you will soar out of your present state of consciousness to higher realms, to intercourse with other, loftier beings and currents. You will constantly be led to greater heights of nobleness and sublime understanding; you will frequent regions where other, more beautiful, more highly evolved entities dwell, and they will lavish all their treasures on you. And so you will go, up and up, blossoming and becoming stronger and stronger.

You must understand the mechanism at work here: each of your thoughts and feelings, every wish or gesture has a relation of affinity with entities and elements of other regions which are attracted to you. That is why I insist so much on this point: whether or not God's Kingdom is actually established on earth is not your problem. Don't worry about it! What matters is that it be established in you. That is all-important.

The establishment of God's Kingdom on earth does not depend on us. God Himself will decree it when the time comes. That is His responsibility; the work of preparing for it is ours. And this means that even if we doubt, even if we do not believe that it will ever happen, we still have to work for it. You may doubt, you may be sceptical: it does not matter. You have a right not to believe in the outcome. But you have no right to stop working. So, there you are: doubt to your heart's content... but go on working and the Kingdom of God will infiltrate into you: that is enough. When a great many people have established the Kingdom within themselves as a continuous state of mind and soul it will be contagious. Everyone will follow their example and before very long the Kingdom of God will have become a fact, a reality for all.

The problem at the moment is ourselves: it is we who have to work, we who have to exert ourselves. When we have done our share the Cosmic Laws will take care of actually establishing the Kingdom as a concrete reality. Thousands upon thousands of spirits have already been at work at it for a very long time now. We are not pioneers in this field! And they never stop insisting on the idea and hoping and praying that it will soon come true. But that is all they can do now: hope and insist. Now it is entirely up to the living. Those who have already left this world can influence the minds and hearts of the living, but they no longer have any control over the material world, whereas the living have tremendous power over matter because they are in constant contact with it. This is why Heaven needs workers, highly developed human beings, to participate in this grandiose scheme: the establishment of God's Kingdom on earth.

So, as you see, these few words: "Seek ye first the Kingdom of God and His justice" constitutes one of the key passages of the Gospels and demands your closest attention. But there are other phrases in the Gospel which are exceedingly important too. This one, for example: "My Father is always at his work... and I, too, am working." Then again, "I am the light of the world" and "I am the resurrection and the life." You must work with light to the point of being able, one day, to say those words of yourself. The point is that it is important to choose the passages in the Gospels which speak of the highest, most sublime ideal and work with them. Some people would rather choose a commandment: "Thou shalt not steal.... Thou shalt not covet thy neighbour's wife...." But that does not really get you very far! So, all right, you are not in the habit of stealing or of coveting somebody else's wife, but how much have you really gained

on the spiritual level by meditating on these
commandments? No. We have to concentrate
on the Kingdom of God, to wish and long for
that divine state of perfection: all the other virtues and qualities are included in it in all their
fullness. And not only must we wish and long for
it but we have to do everything we possibly can
to make it come about.

Even if you are weak, ill-prepared, not at all
learned... none of that matters. All comers are
welcome when it comes to working for the Kingdom of God. Even if you contribute only one
stone to the edifice, what counts is that you are
doing your share and you will be paid the same
wages as the workers of the first hour. It says so
in the Gospel: the workers of the eleventh hour
received the same wages as those who had arrived early in the morning. Possibly you arrived
before anyone else.... Yes, but if you have
worked slowly, without much conviction or ardour you will not reap a very rich reward. In this
work it is the quality of your participation that
counts, not the number of hours you put in.
Some people arrived a bit late perhaps, but they
have worked with tremendous zeal and enthusiasm, and that is what counts most in the divine
world: your ardour, the intensity of your feelings. Men will be rewarded in proportion to the
intensity of their thoughts and love.

# 5

# "ON EARTH AS IT IS IN HEAVEN"

# I

Over the centuries a great many religions, philosophies and schools of thought have made their appearance amongst men and, basically, they can be divided into two categories: those which encourage men to shun the material world and those which, on the contrary, would have them engage all their energies in this world.

The principal philosophy which teaches men to detach themselves from the world, on the pretext that it is imperfect and can offer only pain and suffering, is that of Buddhism, and Buddhism has had a good deal of influence on other spiritual movements. As for the philosophy which enjoins men to cling to the world and look for happiness and the satisfaction of all their wants in the world, that is, of course, materialism.

"And what about Christianity?" you may ask. "Which category does it come into?" Well, that is a very good question because no one really knows: Christianity is not at all clear on the subject. Then, too, we have to make the distinction between the Christianity we know, today, and Christ's philosophy: they are two very different things.

Christianity could be the true philosophy of Christ if Christians understood that, without ceasing to be spiritualist beings, they should also tend the earth and work on it, by means of their thoughts, feelings and actions, so that it may become a garden lovely enough for God to walk in. Neither those who cling to the material world nor those whose one idea is to escape from it will ever be happy. The third solution, which is the true philosophy of Christ and all the great Initiates and, consequently, which is our philosophy too, is not to escape from the world and seek refuge in Heaven, but to become so steeped in the things of Heaven that we are able to bring Heaven down to earth and make the earth into a Garden of Eden, the Kingdom of God. A truly spiritual person, a true Christian does not despise the earth, he endeavours to transform it.

This is why I say that the prayer Jesus gave his disciples, the Lord's Prayer, sums up the whole of his philosophy. It is an all-embracing programme: "Our Father, which art in heaven, hallowed be thy name, thy Kingdom come. Thy

will be done on earth as it is in heaven...."
Buddhists have never taught that the earth
should be like heaven. On the contrary, they
have always yearned to leave the earth behind
and escape to Heaven, and they have certainly
never thought it was possible to transform the
earth. But Jesus was different; he believed that,
one day, men would unite to organize the world
and make it a fit dwelling place for the spirits of
light. He believed this and planned a whole programme to be carried out.

It is not enough to repeat: "Thy will be done
on earth as it is in heaven." That will not solve
any problems. It is we who, by our work, have to
carry out the programme. It is no use thinking
that if we fold our arms and meditate about de-
serting the world we shall persuade the Lord to
come and put everything right again. That
prayer will be granted only by the work of each
one of us.

If some Christians, who have been influenced
by other doctrines, long to leave the world...
well, that is their business. But they must realize
that Jesus never taught any such thing. It is a notion that was introduced into Christian thinking
at a later date. For no religion keeps its original
purity forever: it is always influenced by other
philosophies and religions.

Jesus' religion is a religion of the most lofty

spirituality orientated toward a task to be accomplished here, on earth. As for all those who have taken refuge in convents or monasteries, or in desert caves... of course all that was very admirable, but most of them were only interested in their own souls, they wanted to save their souls... and that is not love. That is not the Teaching of Christ.

Jesus brought to the world a doctrine of love and brotherliness which existed in no other religion. When he said, "Jerusalem, Jerusalem... how often would I have gathered thy children together, even as a hen gathereth her chickens under her wings..." he implied a life of brotherliness and love amongst men. And when he prayed that everything on earth should be as it was in Heaven, it is because, in Heaven, all creatures are as one : they understand each other, they love each other, they are in communion with each other, whereas here, on earth, they are separated, divided against each other, hostile. In such contitions it is clear that the order that prevails in Heaven is very far from being established on earth.

In the Emerald Tablet, Hermes Trismegistus says, "That which is below is like to that which is above." In other words, what is here below, on this earth, is like what is above, in Heaven.

Now, if we compare this with what Jesus says in the Our Father, "Thy will be done on earth as it is in heaven", we could say that Hermes states something as a fact whereas Jesus expresses a wish, a prayer. In reality, though, the two phrases concern different regions. When Hermes Trismegistus says that what is below is like what is above, he is speaking of the three kingdoms: mineral, vegetable and animal, which are a faithful reflection of the world above. But minerals, plants and animals have no free will, whereas men have, and this is why men are the only creatures who do not respect the law of correspondences. The world of man is the only exception: one cannot say of it that "That which is below is like to that which is above." It would not be true. So Jesus prayed that it would become true: "Thy will be done on earth – in other words: in the world of man – as it is in heaven."

Hermes Trismegistus possessed the "science of the three worlds", hence his name "Trismegistus" which means "Thrice Great" and commentators have always understood the "three worlds" to be the divine, the astral and the physical worlds. This is true, but Hermes also spoke of the mineral world from which he obtained the Philosophers' Stone, the vegetable world which gave him the quintessence known as the Elixir of everlasting life and the animal world, from which he obtained the power of the magic wand. As for the world of men, this was Jesus' special domain. When we say "Thy will be done on earth as it is in heaven", we must, at the same time, strive to be in harmony with the cosmic order.

Unfortunately, Christians have never interpreted the words this way. They repeat them, but in doing so they feel in no way obliged to put them into practice and establish God's Kingdom within themselves. They seem to expect it to drop into their laps, ready-made, so that they can benefit from it. That is not right! If that is our attitude God's Kingdom will never come. In fact, if it is not already here, it is because men do not know how to wish for it or ask for it. If they knew this it would already be with us.... Do you really want to know how to ask for God's Kingdom to come? Exactly as I have been saying: each individual must begin by establishing it in himself. Once that is done it will be established in the world around us. This is the only way the Kingdom of God can come on earth. How could it possibly come into men and women whose minds and hearts are filled with disorder, egotism and evil? Exterior transformations can only take place once there has been an inner transformation, because the exterior, visible world is a reflection, a materialization, a physical manifestation of the spiritual world. Nothing can be made manifest outwardly which does not already exist inwardly. How can a stupid man achieve anything intelligent? Intelligence is not in him.

The Kingdom of God cannot exist outwardly until and unless it exists inwardly. A whole is made up of multiple elements: if you eliminate the elements, the whole, too, will disappear. The Kingdom of God on earth is an integrated social order consisting of disinterested, enlightened human beings inspired by the same lofty ideal. If these constituent elements are not present how can that perfect order exist? The whole can only exist as a result of the character, qualities and virtues of all the individuals. What is truly amazing is that human beings still have not understood this!

Most people behave as though their only reason for being on earth is to eat and drink and have a good time or, alternatively, depending upon their point of view, to suffer and be thoroughly unhappy. The truth is that they are here in order to work at one great common venture... but they do not know it. They have forgotten that their mission is to manifest the Divinity concealed within them, to become like God Himself.

In the higher spheres, matter is so subtle that it is instantly obedient to the commands of thought, imagination and will. You can do what you like with it. Think of a complex dance figure or a difficult physical exercise, for example: in your imagination you can execute it to perfection... but as soon as you try to do so on the physical plane you run into trouble! You have to practice an exercise over and over again until you can do it perfectly. And this is true in all areas of activity: mental constructs are not enough, there has to be physical realization too. Besides, if human beings confined themselves to the subtler regions where it is so easy to create they would not grow or develop very much. That is why they are here, on earth: to work on opaque, coarse, unrefined matter and transform it until it glows from within with the beauty and glory of God Himself.

When man's being vibrates in perfect unison with the divine world he will, at last, be a reflection of perfect beauty, light and intelligence. And since the earth – by which I mean this planet earth – partakes of the same nature as man's physical body, it, too, will be transformed and become subtle, vibrant and luminous. Even the plants, fruit and flowers of the earth will be transformed because of the transformation in the lives of men. Once men understand what they have to do, first and foremost, to transform themselves, then the earth and everything on it will be changed. Only then will the earth truly become the dwelling-place of Heaven.

But where are the workers willing to commit themselves? Human beings have other things in mind, so they are going to have to return to earth over and over again until, at last, they turn it into a Garden of Eden. And when this is done they will be free to move on to other planets and leave this earth to the animals which also have to grow and evolve. Perhaps this surprises you.... In any case, in the meantime, man's task is here, on this earth. Admittedly, it is not easy: there is a lot of suffering and unhappiness here. But whose fault is that? It is our own fault! Besides, just because it hurts is no reason to run away from the battlefield. Heaven has no room for deserters. Perhaps you will protest: "But that's all I'm really interested in: Paradise on earth, a state of heavenly bliss. I love peace, light and beauty." So much the better! It will certainly be noted in your favour... but it is not enough. The groundwork has still not been done. Your task is not finished yet.

This earth is made of such dense, crude matter that it will take millions and millions of creatures to transform it. But the question is: "How? How can they transform it?" My answer

is, "By eating it!" Yes, I mean it. This is something else that science has not yet discovered:
why we eat. It is the earth we are eating.... Oh, it
has been dressed up a bit and made to look
appetizing in the form of fruit and vegetables,
but it is still earth. And that earth has to go
through us: it has to be swallowed, digested and
excreted, swallowed, digested and excreted over
and over again until every particle is charged
with the emanations and vibrations of our human thoughts and sentiments. Once the earth is
impregnated in this way it will become luminous
and transparent. Of course, we receive something from the earth as it goes through us, but it
also receives something from us: our feelings
and thoughts, something of our vitality. That is
why it is no longer exactly the same as it was in
the distant past. It has already evolved a great
deal; it is subtler and more intelligent because of
all the human beings who have lived and worked
on the planet and influenced it.

From now on, each one of you must bear in
mind that you have to work at transforming the
earth and, one day, you will hear the Lord de-
clare: "Well done, my good and faithful servants, you have done good work in my fields!
Enter now into my Kingdom of glory and de-
light." In the Gospels did not Jesus talk about
labourers who were sent to work in the vine-

yard? Well, that is what we are: farm labourers. And what have we planted? Where have we been working? You know the parable of the talents that a man entrusted to his servants. Well, the idea is the same: the servants who had earned interest on their talents were rewarded, whereas the one who had hoarded his only talent was punished. This wicked, feckless servant symbolizes those who are only interested in having a good time and living for themselves. That attitude is a far cry from the philosophy Christ taught. He taught that all the talents and possibilities the Lord has given us must be put to good use for the benefit of all men.

The whole meaning of life is evolution, the transformation of matter. What shapes and forms things will eventually take is another question: the only thing we need to know here and now is that everything makes sense, there is a master plan, a law propelling the whole of creation forward on its evolutionary path. It follows, therefore, that those who contribute to the evolutionary process will be helped and supported. Everything that exists has to evolve: even minerals. The evolution of the mineral world is, no doubt, imperceptible but it is none the less real. A hidden force in the mineral world is constantly striving to bring to light all its potential, inherent qualities and virtues. Precious stones and metals are the most advanced mineral forms and they emanate something which can be beneficial to men. Plants evolve also and the more advanced they are, the greater the curative, nutritional and beneficial properties of their flowers and fruit. And the same is true of animals and human beings, and even of the solar system.

Evolution is the law of life. Evolution, that is, meaning growth and development to the point of perfection. And if Jesus told us to be perfect as our Heavenly Father is perfect, it was because he knew that perfection was the ultimate goal of evolution.

## II

The whole of creation is the result of the combined action of spirit and matter. That is what the universe is made of: spirit and matter. For materialists who abhor the word "spirit", we can substitute the term energy, or force, for the spirit is a force. The only problem is that if we say force instead of spirit, we are depriving ourselves of the particular properties of the spirit: intelligence, consciousness and love. In any case, no one can deny that everything in the universe revolves around two poles of reality, whether you call them spirit and matter, force and matter or the masculine and feminine principles.

Science is concerned principally with the evolutionary process by which living species have differentiated and become organized by acquiring new properties and aptitudes. In other words, science has been concerned exclusively with the upward movement, the movement of matter toward the spirit. What has never been understood is that the upward, evolutionary movement was preceded by an involutionary movement, and if scientists have never realized this it is because involution is something which does not come within their field of observation, it takes place on a higher level, but owing to this gap in their knowledge their conclusions are, necessarily, inexact.

Initiatic Science teaches that all evolutionary movement is preceded by its opposite : what we call involution, which is the downpouring of the spirit into matter. Evolution could not take place at all if the spirit had no part in it, for it is the spirit that contains life and consciousness. It is the spirit that sets matter, forms and all created beings on the upward path to perfection. It is important, therefore, to understand that there can be no evolution without prior involution. To believe that forms have evolved all by themselves, without previously benefiting from involution, the descent of the spirit, makes no sense at all. The notion of involution and evolution can be symbolized by two triangles : the triangle with the point turned downwards symbolizes the spirit which comes down into matter to breathe life into it, and the one pointing upwards symbolizes matter which tends to rise, to evolve, in order to unite and become one with the spirit.

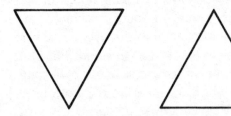

The symbolism of the two triangles can also be applied to the spiritual life: the upward-looking triangle symbolizes those who espouse the movement of matter. They have a tendency to abandon the world with all its activities and duties, and this leads to certain deviations. These people have to learn to work with the downward-looking triangle, the triangle of the spirit, the triangle of realization and manifestation on the physical level. What is important, now, is no longer to move upwards, but downwards. Probably a lot of "mystical" people will exclaim in horror: "Oh, but this is terrible! It's when you go down that you lose yourself. No one has ever said we should do that. It's just the opposite: you have to rise and disentangle yourself from the world." Well, have it your own way, but that is not the attitude Jesus taught in the Lord's Prayer: "Thy Kingdom come, thy will be done on earth as it is in heaven."

The time is coming when we must no longer try to save our souls by taking refuge in Heaven. That attitude was, no doubt, acceptable at some point. It enabled men to discover some very important aspects of the spiritual life. But we should no longer seek to save our own souls. We have to commit ourselves to the glorious task of bringing Heaven down to earth. Perhaps you will wonder how you can possibly do such a thing; it may seem that it is simply not in your power to do so. You would be wrong: it is in your power and the triangle of the spirit shows you how it can be done. Granted, a disciple has to reach for Heaven, but once there, he has to try and bring back to earth the light of Heaven, the love and the power and the purity of Heaven. He has to fill his own soul with this light, love, power and purity until he overflows with it and can pour it out on others around him. In this way, after years and years of striving, he succeeds in bringing spirit and matter together again and attains the fullness of perfection symbolized by the two, interlaced triangles known as Solomon's Seal.

A lot of esoteric books talk about Solomon's Seal, but very few of them have any grasp of the depth and magic power of this symbol. Its power is derived from the conjunction and interpenetration of the two triangles, symbols of the two principles.

Nowadays we see a lot of extreme tendencies coming to the surface. On the one hand there are the "progressive" countries which are highly developed and well organized in all the technical, economic and social fields. They do everything imaginable to improve their earthly condition but they completely ignore the claims of the spirit. And then there are others which have such a rich spiritual tradition that the material dimension is almost totally neglected. And here you have millions and millions of people living in filth, destitution and disease. I cannot approve either type. Both tendencies are necessary: we must always keep in contact with Heaven but, at the same time, we must work for the world.

You will perhaps feel that you prefer to work for Heaven. That is very understandable, but

don't you realize that Heaven does not need
you? It is so lavishly endowed already, so overflowing with riches! What could you possibly
add to all that? No, it is down here, on earth,
that you are needed. It is time, now, to change
your tactics! I do not mean that you should begin to neglect or turn your back on Heaven, God
forbid! On the contrary, you have to maintain
close ties with Heaven if you want to have something to give to others. Because, you see, if you
are not in close contact with Heaven, you will
not have access to all its wealth, and then what
would you have to distribute around you?

In some of the poorer countries of the world
a lot of the men leave their homes to go abroad
and earn money for the families. And you can
do the same thing: you can go abroad and earn
money to buy food for your family. I am speaking symbolically, as you realize. By "abroad" I
mean the celestial world above, and you can go
there by means of prayer, meditation, contemplation and so on. This is what I do: every day I
abandon you and go abroad to earn gold, so that
when I come back I have something to give you.
Why cling to your family and friends all the
time? Because you love them? No, I don't believe it. People do not really love their families,
or, at least, they love them very badly. They let
them die of starvation because they have nothing

to give them to feed their hearts and souls. Is that love?

You have to be able to dwell in Heaven but you must never be content to stay there. Let me give you an example: you have had a beautiful idea which makes you very happy. You can feel that it is really a good idea. This means that your idea has already moved from your mind and reached the level of your feelings. But, obviously, you cannot leave it at that; it is only when you begin to express it in words and actions that the normal process is complete. Do you think painters, musicians and poets are content to keep their ideas in their heads? Certainly not. They turn them into works of art. Then why should you be content to leave your good ideas up in the air, in the form of thoughts and feelings and never bring them down to earth? It is necessary to give concrete form to things. And this is just as necessary in the area of spirituality and religion. Religion, for a great many people, is exclusively in the mind or the heart with the result that their behaviour is often in direct contradiction to what they think and believe. They simply have not understood how Cosmic Intelligence conceives things. First we have to think of something, next we have to wish for it and, finally, we have to set to work to embody it in matter.

When a boy meets a girl and falls in love, it is not long before he tries to get close enough to her to kiss her. Why do you think he was not content to think about her and enjoy the feeling of his love? Ah, you see! It is amazing how men and women seem to know exactly what to do in this area! They follow the normal process envisaged by Cosmic Intelligence. And where the things of the spirit are concerned, also, we must not neglect to put them into actual practice, to give them concrete form by our gestures, attitudes and work.

Some of you may be thinking, "That's all very fine, but you're contradicting yourself. You're always criticizing materialists for being interested only in the things of this earth, and saying that when they get over to the other side they won't be able to keep any of the things they've acquired here, on earth. And now you're saying we have to do exactly what they do." No, I am not contradicting myself, for it is one thing to be attached only to money and material possessions, it is quite another to work for the realization on earth of all the splendours of Heaven.

And besides, do you really believe that materialists are interested in improving the world? Not in the least! Their only concern is to get rich, themselves, even if they have to despoil, pollute and destroy the world in doing so. I am afraid the earth does not benefit much from their activity. Spiritual people, on the other hand, contribute something to the earth and when they leave it they are robed in all the lovely things they have achieved in the world of light. This is how they create their own future.

We bring you a new philosophy, a different code of behaviour, a new way of thinking, acting and manifesting oneself. The old way of looking at things was good for each, separate individual, but useless for the community of men. Now we have entered an era in which men must no longer work only for their own betterment, but for that of the whole world, for the whole of humanity. Immortality is above. Light is above. Harmony is above. Peace, beauty and all that is pure and subtle is above. But why should all that not become incarnate below, on the physical plane and, first and foremost, in our physical bodies? Why should the life of the celestial sphere above not impregnate our physical bodies? Why should its radiance not shine through us? When this comes to pass, then, yes: the Kingdom of God will come and each one of us will be a lamp, a sun, a source. We must accept what the triangle of involution, the triangle of the spirit, teaches us and cease to follow exclusively the teaching of the triangle of matter.

Matter tends to move upwards. The spirit

has a tendency to move downwards. And men
and women, when they join in a loving embrace,
repeat and reflect the same phenomenon: the
man faces downwards and the woman upwards.
Human beings are simply conforming to principles established from the beginning of time by
Cosmic Intelligence: matter, tending towards
the spiritual and the spirit tending to manifest itself in matter, come together in space to fuse
into one in the act of creation. All men's acts are
symbolic. All men's acts are eloquent and philosophical, but they themselves understand nothing of all this. We must bring the spirit down
into matter. In your prayers and meditations,
therefore, call on the light, the spirit, divine
power; call on it and picture it flowing into you
and impregnating every cell in your body. And
when you have worked with this method for
years, one day you will feel that Heaven, light
and love have filled your being. When this happens it will be far easier for you to stimulate
others along the same lines and far easier, also,
to help them on their way. Whereas if, on the
pretext of being "spiritual" you shrivel up like a
piece of old parchment, not only will you be no
use to anyone else, but you will put them off
spirituality for good.

The spirit must come down into this world.
When the spirit has impregnated matter here,

below, then the fruit of their union, the child, will be born... and the child is the Kingdom of God in all its beauty. So this is the new way I spoke of: to bring all the beauty and blessings, all the light and peace of Heaven itself down to earth, down to our own "earth", our own physical bodies, first of all, and then to the whole world, the whole of humanity.

There, I think that is clear now: instead of dreaming and losing yourself in the joys of Nirvana, instead of feasting and rejoicing with the chosen few high above this world, remember that you can bring Heaven down to earth, that its light will spread over the whole world, that you yourself will be a light on this earth... what more glorious venture could there be?

# 6

## "HE THAT EATETH MY FLESH AND DRINKETH MY BLOOD, HATH ETERNAL LIFE"

As you know, the Communion rites observed to this day in the Christian churches originated in the last meal that Jesus shared with his disciples. "And as they were eating, Jesus took bread, and blessed it, and brake it, and gave it to the disciples and said, Take, eat; this is my body. And he took a cup, and gave thanks, and gave it to them, saying, Drink ye all of it; for this is my blood...."

In the Gospel of St. John we read that Jesus also said: "I am the living bread which came down from heaven: if any man eat of this bread, he shall live for ever: and the bread that I will give is my flesh, which I will give for the life of the world.... Verily, verily, I say unto you, Except ye eat the flesh of the Son of man, and drink his blood, ye have no life in you. Whoso eateth my flesh, and drinketh my blood, hath eternal life; and I will raise him up at the last day. For my flesh is meat indeed, and my blood is drink indeed. He that eateth my flesh, and drinketh my blood, dwelleth in me, and I in him. As the living Father has sent me, and I live by the Father: so he that eateth me, even he shall live by me."

The symbols of bread and wine, presented as the flesh and blood of Christ, are to be found in all forms of Initiation. In the book of Genesis we read of Abraham's encounter with Melchizedek, King of Salem: "And the king of Sodom went out to meet Abram after his return from the slaughter of Chedorlaomer, and of the kings that were with him, at the valley of Shaveh, which is the king's dale. And Melchizedek, king of Salem brought forth bread and wine: and he was the high priest of the most high God. And he blessed him, and said, Blessed be Abram of the most high God, possessor of heaven and earth: And blessed be the most high God, which hath delivered thine enemies into thy hand. And Abram gave him tithes of all."

The name Melchizedek, which means "king of justice", comes from the Hebrew words for king: *melek*, and justice: *tsedek*. And the name of his kingdom, Salem, has the same root as the Hebrew word for peace: *shalom*. Melchizedek is the king of justice and peace. He is a very mysterious figure and we know very little about him. Only the great Initiates know anything about him. There is one other mention of Melchizedek in the Bible and that is in St. Paul's Epistle to the Hebrews. St. Paul writes: "For this Melchizedek, king of Salem, priest of the most high God, who met Abraham returning from the slaughter of the kings, and blessed him; To whom also Abraham gave a tenth part of all; first being by interpretation King of justice, and after that also King of Salem, which is King of peace; without father, without mother, without descent, having neither beginning of days, nor end of life; but made like unto the Son of God; abideth a priest continually." The Holy Eucharist, instituted by Jesus, reproduced the offering of bread and wine that Melchizedek made to Abraham. In addition, St. Paul says, that Jesus was "a high priest for ever after the order of Melchizedek."

Bread and wine, that is: wheat and grapes and, by extension, all food, are symbols of Christ, the Word, because they are all fruits of the sun. It is the sun's rays that ripen wheat and grapes and all the fruits and grains of the earth. All the nourishment we draw from the earth, everything we eat and drink, are the body and blood of Christ, for the love, light and life transmitted to us through the sun are the very love, light and life of Christ himself, which condense and take shape on earth in the form of vegetation and fruit.

"He who eats my flesh and drinks my blood has eternal life." If you can grasp the full significance of these words they will take you a long way. Jesus was saying: "If you eat the fire which comes from me and which is love; if you drink my light, which is wisdom, you will have eternal life." He had said the same thing, in other words to Nicodemus: "Except a man be born of water and of the spirit (or fire), he cannot enter into the Kingdom of God." Flesh and blood, fire and water are symbols, but on different levels, of the same two principles revealed to Abraham by Melchizedek in the gift of bread and wine. Bread and wine do not amount to much as a gift, but in offering them to Abraham, the priest of the most high God was making him a truly prodigious gift: he was initiating him into the true significance of the masculine and feminine principles.

As it is very difficult for human beings to grasp the great mysteries of the cosmos, concrete images such as bread, wine and hosts have been used to bring them down from the sublime world which is their true home, to our level, here on earth. But it is high time men reached a more profound understanding of these symbols. Bread and wine are solar symbols because they represent two of the sun's special characteristics: light and life-giving warmth. The warmth of the sun is love. Its light is wisdom. So what Jesus was saying was: "If you eat my flesh (wisdom) and drink my blood (love), you will have eternal life."

Christians communicate with consecrated hosts, but are they any better for doing so? Whereas someone who communicates with the sun, with that great host, as it rises in the morning sky, and drinks the light flowing from it in such abundance, enters into eternal life. Jesus' words must be understood on a far higher level; we always look for their meaning on too low a level. Now all these symbols and representations are very good as far as they go: I have no intention of demolishing them. For the time being they are still useful and necessary. But one day people will realize that they are not really efficacious, for in spite of them, they are still just as weak, ignorant and cowardly, just as vengeful and jealous, just as ready to blacken their neighbour's name as they ever were.

Over the last 2 000 years untold numbers of Christians have eaten wagon-loads of hosts and drunk barrels of wine without gaining eternal life and, unfortunately, without the slightest apparent improvement in them. For the only way to attain eternal life is to eat the light and warmth of Christ. And Christ is in the sun, he is the spirit of the sun. Yes, that light flowing from the sun and giving birth to all forms of life on earth, that

light whose true nature is still a mystery to us, is
Christ, the spirit of Christ. The light of the sun is
a living spirit and it is by means of this light that
Christ is always with us, present, active, constantly at work.

Of course, Christ is a far greater entity than
the sun. He is the Son of God, Second Person of
the Blessed Trinity. And nor does he manifest
himself only through the sun. There are innu-
merable suns in the universe and most of them
are much bigger and more brilliant than ours.

Christ is in all of them; he is everywhere in
the universe, but for us human beings who live
on the planet earth he manifests himself in our
sun.

There is a tradition that Zoroaster asked the
god, Ahura-Mazda, how the first man was nour-
ished and Ahura-Mazda replied: "He ate fire
and drank light." And why should we not learn
to eat fire and drink light, too, and rediscover
the perfection of that first man? When you are
watching the sun rise, practice eating and drink-
ing it. Imagine that you are breathing it in, that
living sunlight courses through all the cells of
your body, imbuing them with strength, purity
and life.

Every day you go and meditate in the presence of the rising sun: there it is, before your
gaze, sending out light particles of the greatest

purity into space. What is to prevent you from summoning up all your powers of concentration and sloughing off your old, shabby, worn-out particles and replacing them with brand-new particles straight from the sun? This can be an extremely effective exercise! Strive with all your heart and soul to capture these divine particles and incorporate them into yourself; little by little, thanks to the sun, you will completely renew the whole fabric of your being. You will begin to think and behave like true children of God.

The religion of the future will be the solar religion: because, every day, the sun gives us the means we need to communicate with the Godhead, to eat the body and drink the blood of Christ.

# 7

# "FATHER, FORGIVE THEM, FOR THEY KNOW NOT WHAT THEY DO"

A lot of people read the Gospels and write commentaries on them, but as often as not they are very far from having penetrated Jesus' mind. This is because one always has a tendency to interpret other people's words and actions in the light of one's own, limited point of view and even in the light of one's own faults and failings. As I often say, if we want to know what someone really meant we have to be able to get inside his head. There are ways of finding out what people long-dead meant in their sayings or writings and those who know and apply these methods all come to the same conclusions. But those who do not know or use these methods never manage to agree with each other. There are as many different interpretations as there are commentators, and nowadays people are so sick of all these conflicting explanations, even of the Gospels, that they do not want to listen to any of it anymore... and that is only to be expected.

Take just one example: for 2000 years now, people have quoted Jesus' words as he hung from the cross, "Father, forgive them for they know not what they do." All the commentators insist on the need to forgive, telling us that we must forgive as Jesus did. So, for the last 2000 years, all those who have taken these words to heart have been trying to forgive their enemies or anyone who has done them an injury. But how is it they have never been very successful in doing so? It is simply because Jesus possessed a secret and so long as we do not know that secret, even if we want to take him as our model, we shall never be capable of forgiveness. It is not enough to want to follow the example Jesus gave us. As long as we are not really in communication with him by means of our knowledge and understanding of what he knew and understood, he will always be remote and inaccessible and we shall never be able to imitate him. And of course, a lot of people think he was able to forgive because he was the Christ, the Son of God, whereas we, who are only human, shall never be able to forgive.

Now, what I want to explain to you today is how to forgive those who have injured you. Perhaps some of you will say that you are not at all eager to forgive.... Well, that is your business, you can do as you please. But you had better

realize that you will have to bear the burden of
your attitude and it is not a light burden to bear.
It is a bitter, corrosive thing, a grudge, which
will torment you and poison your existence and
you would do well to try and get rid of it. However, as it is not recommended to get rid of it by
killing your enemy, it is much better to forgive
him... and I shall explain how you can do that.

First of all, let's analyse Jesus' words:
"Father, forgive them for they know not what
they do." I wonder why these words have never
been correctly analysed. "Father, forgive them
for...." It seems that Jesus was explaining to God
that He should forgive them and even why He
should forgive them! Is that what they mean?
Can anyone teach God something He does not
already know? Why did Jesus feel the need to
add "for they know not what they do"? Surely
He knew that? Doesn't God know that human
beings are ignorant and stupid and unconscious
of the gravity of their acts? Did He need Jesus to
tell Him that? And then, too, instead of saying
"I forgive them", he said, "Father, forgive
them". Why should God forgive them? He had
nothing to do with all that; it was not He who
was being crucified, it was Jesus.

Ah, but it is here that we find the Key to
forgiveness; in the words: "Father, forgive
them". In pronouncing these words Jesus allied

himself, as it were, with God and, in so doing, he placed himself on a higher level than his enemies and executioners. Seeing them from that vantage point he could only pity them: their conduct proved that they were unintelligent, unenlightened and wretchedly poor, for to be deprived of light is to be deprived of everything worthwhile. Once he had moved up onto that higher plane, therefore, he saw their wretchedness so clearly that it was as though he really had no need any longer to forgive them. So, you see, this formula was simply a psychological method by means of which Jesus transformed his own inner attitude. Perhaps you don't agree. Perhaps you are saying to yourself, "That's not it at all. Jesus knew that God was terrible and implacable and that He would punish his executioners, so he begged Him to spare them." No! Jesus taught that God is Love. How could he possibly think, all of a sudden, that he ought to protect these men from God's wrath? If he had thought that, it means he considered himself better than the Lord, he thought he was more magnanimous, more generous and merciful... but that is unthinkable!

"Father, forgive them for they know not what they do" is a formula Jesus used to conquer and transform the last, tiniest drop of rancour that may have been lurking in his heart.

You are very mistaken, you know, if you believe that Jesus was always meek, indulgent and kind! Look at the way he treated the Pharisees and Sadducees. He called them all kinds of terrible names: hypocrites, blind fools, whited sepulchres, snakes, brood of vipers.... There was undoubtedly something in his make-up that was capable of being unforgiving. Yes, but he *wanted* to forgive. He wanted to rid himself, down to the last tiny atom, of all hostility towards human beings, including his enemies. He had taught that men should love their enemies so, of course, he had to be the first to do so. And it was that prayer, "Father, forgive them for they know not what they do", which gave him, instantaneously, the power to forgive everything.

If you try to explain these words in any other way everything becomes more complicated. We would be obliged to conclude that Jesus did not really have much faith in God's love and thought he had to encourage Him to be kind and forgiving. But this supposes that Jesus considered himself better than God, which would be unconscionable pride. No. Jesus was using a purely psychological formula and it had a magical effect, for it placed him on such a high level and his enemies on such a low level, that he succeeded in finding it in his heart to pity them. When one sees so clearly how ignorant, brutish and wretched human beings really are, one has no inclination to trample them down even further. And that is what it means to be noble. If you are noble you do not attack someone smaller or weaker than yourself.

Jesus had such nobility of love, wisdom and power that he was capable of forgiveness. If he had not forgiven his executioners, he could have blasted them out of existence with a bolt of lightning: he had it in his power to do so. But he forgave them precisely because he did not want to behave like all those who had gone before him: they acted according to the precepts of justice for they were the servants of justice. But justice knows no forgiveness: it is an eye for an eye, a tooth for a tooth. But Jesus had come to teach love, pity, the forgiveness of offences and that is why, before he died, he pleaded in favour of his enemies. Once one has truly understood the secret of these words, one can use them oneself and the results are really extraordinary.

Someone who is spiritually indigent and weak is incapable of forgiveness. He wants to revenge himself. In order to forgive those who have injured you, you have to become great-hearted, wealthy, powerful and full of light. Tell yourself, "I can most surely forgive him, poor creature. He's neither enlightened nor noble-minded and he's very ignorant! He doesn't real-

ize what he's letting himself in for. The laws of
divine justice are inexorable and he's bound to
suffer for all the evil he's done. And though I'm
his victim for the moment, I'm so tremendously
privileged to be working for good, for the Kingdom of God, for the light!" If you really believe
this and compare the splendour of your life – because you have chosen to walk the path of good-
ness – with the squalor and gloom in the lives of
those who are unjust and evil, you will be seized
by a profound sentiment of pity. Such an attitude would be totally out of your reach by any
other means, but this way it is easy.

Some of you may say, "But what's the difference between what you describe and the attitude
of the Pharisee when he was praying in the Temple? The Gospel says he thanked God that he
wasn't like other men and, especially, that he
wasn't like that Publican who was standing
humbly at a distance. It's just pride!" No, it is
not at all the same thing: the Pharisee boasted
that he fasted twice a week and gave away a
tenth of all he earned and so on, and that was
why he despised the Publican. He never imagined that the good man was perhaps better than
he. The attitude I am talking about is quite different. What I am saying is that when you have
been the victim of calumny or some other injustice, if you recognize the amazing graces God

has showered on you, if you go over them in
your mind and compare all that abundance with
your enemy's impoverished condition, you will
be forced to conclude that you are extremely
privileged. For the time being, your enemy may
have the upper hand; he may have managed to
do you a great deal of damage, but it is still he
who stands most in need of pity, for wrongdoers
are always in need of pity. One day, divine justice will catch up with him and he will be punished in one way or another. So, you see, this is
quite different from the Pharisee's attitude.

It is excellent to read the Gospels, but it is
very important to understand them in depth, to
understand what was in the mind and heart of
Jesus when he said certain things. In this instance, as we have seen, when he said, "Father,
forgive them for they know not what they do",
he was associating himself with his Father so as
to be capable of forgiving his enemies, the Pharisees and Sadducees. Jesus had such integrity and
honesty it was inevitable that he should antago-
nize the Pharisees and Sadducees whom he criti-
cized and reproved on every possible occasion.
Of course, one could object that he was not exactly tactful or diplomatic. He should have
known that if he denounced people in high
places who were both intelligent and learned, he
was putting himself in a very dangerous posi-

tion. At every opportunity he unmasked them and, even in public, in full hearing of the crowds, he laid bare their failings, saying: "Woe unto you, scribes and Pharisees, hypocrites! for ye shut up the Kingdom of heaven against men: for ye neither go in yourselves, neither suffer ye them that are entering to go in." And he accused them, too, of jostling for the place of honour at their banquets or in the synagogue, of stealing from widows, and so on.

If Jesus had been more prudent in his dealings with the Pharisees and Sadducees they probably would not have avenged themselves so drastically. But he provoked them. We have to admit it, frankly: he goaded them ceaselessly. How could they be expected to accept that without reacting? It was impossible! They deserved everything Jesus said, of course, but he could have badgered them a little less, perhaps. And, of course, the question then is: "Why did he behave like that?" The answer is, quite simply, that he did what he did in order that the Scriptures should be fulfilled, in order to accomplish his mission. If he had not treated the Pharisees as he did, he would not have been crucified and the course of history would have been very different: none of the events which happened after that would have taken place.

So that was the work Jesus had to accomplish

in himself as he was dying, in order to overcome all evil, and he used that formula to enable him to forgive his enemies. No one in the whole history of mankind has ever been totally free of all hostility or antipathy toward another person. It is not possible. Even the greatest, most exalted of men cannot completely avoid negative thoughts and feelings. But the thing is that those great beings know exactly what formulae and methods to use to conquer their weaknesses and transform them. And it is in this that they are meritorious. You must not believe that they are born overflowing with love, understanding, wisdom and all possible virtues. Not a bit of it! They have to acquire all that. Knowledge and power have to be earned. Of course, men arrive in this world with certain qualities gained in previous incarnations, and Jesus was particularly richly endowed and had immense virtues, but there is no doubt that he still had one or two little weaknesses to overcome.

I realize that Christians will never accept this idea because in their eyes it is a slur on Jesus. In point of fact it is just the opposite. For me, Jesus seems all the more extraordinary when I see how he succeeded in overcoming every obstacle. He even conquered that terrible fear that threatened to engulf him in the Garden of Gethsemane. What a struggle; what a battle that was! That

fear was the accumulation of forces lurking in
the human body for thousands of years... and he
conquered them! The sweat of blood ran down
his face as he prayed to his Father, "Oh, my
Father, if it be possible, let this cup pass from
me" and then, without a pause, he added, "Nevertheless, not as I will, but as thou will." Later,
hanging on the cross, he cried out, saying, "Eli,
Eli, lama sabachthani?" which means "My
God, my God, why hast thou forsaken me?" For
Jesus to say such a thing, for him to feel as
though he had been abandoned by God, what
must he have gone through, what must have
been his agony? In fact, of course, God had not
abandoned him, but that impression of being
forsaken by God can be experienced even by the
very greatest Initiates. After that, Jesus recap-
tured the serenity of fulfillment and light and
died, saying, "Father, into thy hands I commend
my spirit." You must not think that when I talk
like this I am in any way belittling the majesty of
Jesus. Not in the least! Jesus is very great in my
estimation, far greater than many people believe
him to be, even practicing Christians who still
do not really understand who he was. Yes, for
me, Jesus is very great in spite of the fact that I
make the distinction between Jesus and the
Christ.

Man has two natures: the lower nature

which I call the personality, and a higher nature which I call the individuality. If we know about man's two natures it will help us to understand the different states a human being can go through. Usually people get it all mixed up, and Christians talk about "Jesus" or "Christ" without differentiating between the two. Jesus was the man; the man who lived in Palestine at a given point in time; Christ is the divine principle who dwelt in that man and manifested itself through the medium of his humanity. Unfortunately, even the greatest Initiate cannot manifest, only and always, his divine nature. So, when Jesus was disheartened and weary, it was the man, his personality, who was expressing himself. And the man could also feel rancour, he could be afraid of death, he could feel abandoned by God. How could it have been Christ who expressed anguish at feeling himself abandoned by God? Christ is God; could God abandon Himself?

Sometimes Jesus was tired, sometimes he was hungry or thirsty or sleepy... all that is perfectly normal. But when Christ spoke through him he said: "The Father and I are one"; "I am the living bread that came down from heaven"; "I am the light of the world"; "I am the resurrection and the life"; "I am the vine; you are the branches", and "I am the way, the truth, and the life". I hope this whole question is clear to you now. On the human side deficiencies and failings may well appear; there will be times when the sky is overcast. But when the divine principle manifests itself and speaks, there can be no error nor human frailty. This is your key to understanding the Gospels or any other of the Sacred Books. With this key you will be in a position to judge whether, at any given moment, it was the man expressing himself or the divine principle manifesting itself through the human medium.

And in yourselves, too, the same rule applies. You must be aware of the two natures in you: the human and the divine, and distinguish clearly between them. This is most important. It is precisely on this score that we make most of our mistakes. When the voice of the Divinity speaks in us and gives us good advice, we don't trust it, and we go ahead and do something silly. And then, when the voice of our personality makes itself heard we are all eagerness and attention... and again we do something silly! You must learn to discriminate. You have still not given this question all the attention it deserves: how to distinguish between the two inner voices and which one to listen to. It is of first importance, for the consequences are immense and far-reaching. All of man's misfortunes come

from his failure to discern when it is his personality and when it is his individuality that is seeking to influence him. I have spoken to you time
and again about this, I never stop insisting on it,
but you pay no attention, you brush it aside because it does not really interest you. And yet...
your happiness, your progress and, indeed, your
ultimate success depend on this. To understand
what is going on inside you, where it is coming
from, who is inspiring you... there is nothing
more important.*

When Jesus first spoke of his coming death,
Peter said, "Never, Lord! This shall never happen to you!" and Jesus replied, "Get thee behind me, Satan: thou art a stumbling block to
me: for thou savourest not the things that be of
God, but those that be of men." Here it is obvious that Jesus not only clearly distinguished
the things of God from the things of men, the
individuality from the personality, he was also
quite lucid about the diabolical origin of that
temptation, since he said, "Get thee behind me,
Satan!" The struggle between the individuality
and the personality flared up again in the Garden of Gethsemane and, this time, his personality did not use another human being to try and

* See "Man's two natures, human and divine," the Izvor
Collection, no. 213.

tempt him; it spoke to him directly from within.
And, here again, Jesus commanded his personality to be quiet, and to God he said, "Not as I
will, but as thou wilt." And with that he gained
the upper hand. He had to suffer and die, but he
said, "Thy will be done!" In other words, he rejected the intrigues of his personality and yielded
to the Divinity. Now I ask you, who do you ever
hear explaining things to you in this way? They
say that, when Jesus was in the Garden of
Gethsemane he began to experience, in advance,
the anguish of death... and then, when he was
hanging on the cross, he said, "Father, forgive
them for they know not what they do." But no
one realizes that there is an initiatic truth concealed in each of these particular moments in
Jesus' life. No one notices that there is an important process taking place on the psychic level,
that opposing forces are involved, and no one
sees how the conflict develops nor how the person himself takes part in it.

Jesus' words on the cross, "Father, forgive
them for they know not what they do" become
intelligible only in the light of the conflict between the personality and the individuality.
Don't believe for a moment that it was easy for
Jesus to forgive people who had scorned and
flogged him, who had crowned him with thorns
and nailed him to a cross! But he allied himself

with his individuality and with his Heavenly
Father and, through Him, through the immen-
sity of God's own light and love, he was able to
forgive enemies and executioners. Believe me,
only someone who has worked all his life long to
become one with God, to open himself utterly to
God's coming and in whom God dwells permanently, is capable of forgiving as Jesus forgave.

And you who have had the advantages of this
initiatic school, who have already had the experience through personal contact with the divine
dimension, you should consider yourselves highly privileged and rich. And you should be capable, now, of using that wealth to good purpose. If
someone does you a wrong, you should find it in
your heart to say to yourself, "Lord, how ignorant and feeble the poor fellow is! He really does
deserve to be pitied. In fact he could do with a
little help from me!" This is forgiveness... and
thanks to your forgiveness of him, the whole situation is transformed. Instead of nourishing feelings of resentment and a thirst for revenge, all is
forgiven and forgotten at once. Make a gesture of
generosity and give thanks to God.

If you do not know all this there will always
be some little thing rankling and gnawing at you.
You cannot get rid of the problem by wiping out
your enemy so you have to live with a bitterness
which is always there to poison your existence.

Your enemy is all right : he is free to move about as he pleases, he eats, sleeps and drinks and gets on with his business while you are busy destroying yourself! The only solution is to forgive : but how? If you are too stupid and ignorant to know how, then it becomes an impossible solution, beyond your reach. But now I have given you the key : the knowledge you needed is in your possession.

# 8

## "UNTO HIM THAT SMITETH THEE ON THE ONE CHEEK..."

It says in the Gospels, "Unto him that smiteth thee on the one cheek offer also the other." Now, I trust that the Christians who hear what I am going to say about this will forgive me, for it goes far beyond what they have always imagined. However, the future will show that my interpretation is the right one: some of the moral precepts which were applicable in the past are no longer valid nor useful for us, today; still less will they be adequate in the future.

Jesus' words do not mean that Christians must always accept insults and ill-treatment without reacting in any way. He was not telling us to be totally passive and submissive, to put up with every torment and, in the long run, allow ourselves to be wiped out. True, his words have often been interpreted to mean just that, but I intend to show you that that is not what he meant. Of course, if one does not possess the light there is only one solution: to submit passively and let yourself be destroyed by others.

But that is a code of behaviour for the weak and ignorant and it was certainly not intended to last forever. It has never been decreed that spiritual people and sages, Initiates and Sons of God should be perpetually repressed, persecuted and put to death while their tormentors: imbeciles and corrupt and evil men should triumph over them. For the time being this is still the situation because human beings have lost the divine spark, the strength that comes from the sun, they have lost all warmth, light and life. And having lost all that they are necessarily going to be attacked and ill-treated.

The Gospels also say, "Ye are the salt of the earth: but if the salt have lost its savour... it is thenceforth good for nothing, but to be cast out, and to be trodden under foot of men." So there it is: if you have lost your savour you will be trampled on by men until you get it back again. It has not been decreed that you should be trampled underfoot forever, but when you have deserted God all your strength deserts you, too, and you become an easy prey for the vile and corrupt.

At the time of Jesus, men had reached a stage of development at which they needed to acquire certain qualities and virtues which had been neglected up to then: indulgence, clemency, mercifulness. Before that, the code was one of justice: an eye for an eye, a tooth for a tooth. The new moral code that Jesus introduced, therefore, was designed to encourage human beings to develop the qualities of the heart. Instead of reacting brutally with knives or sticks and stones, they had to learn to respond with nobler, more lofty means: humility, love, patience and magnanimity. That is what Christ's words mean. But Christ was speaking to the men and women of his day and age and what he said for them is not necessarily valid for the rest of time. He is telling us, now, that there is an even better way: "When you are the victim of injustice you should react with such intelligence and potency, with such understanding, light and warmth that your enemy is dazzled and struck dumb... in other words your reaction can transform him. He will not be annihilated nor massacred but re-generated! Instead of dealing death you communicate life to him by bringing him closer to God. If you are capable of doing this, then you are a true hero, a true son of God."

Why should we always let our enemies massacre us and crow over us? We know that we must not kill or hurt anybody, of course, but that is no reason why we should be the eternal underdog. We must learn to defend ourselves by imitating the sun and doing as it does: shine so brightly that even if someone is determined to be vindictive and cruel he will be prevented from doing us any harm by our shield of dazzling, blinding light. In this way you strike your enemies blind, but with a blindness that heals, a blindness that will open their eyes, just as Christ opened Saul's eyes on the road to Damascus when he was bent on massacring the Christians: a ray of light and he fell to the ground, blind. And Saul became Paul. If you could paralyze people in the same way, just for an instant and then heal them again... do you think they would still want to hurt you? The new moral code no longer counsels you to be feeble and at the mercy of all the cruel, violent people in the world, but to become like the sun so that they cannot soil you: you will be out of reach. Or, if they do come close, they will melt like wax in the warmth and radiance of your loving-kindness.

Human beings are not yet properly prepared to use the weapons of light in this way simply because it has never occurred to them that they could do so if they wanted to. They have embraced a brainless philosophy of weakness and impotence on the pretext that Jesus told them to turn the other cheek. Well, you can turn as many cheeks as you like, it will not do you any good and you will not change your enemies the least little bit, that way; they will just go on tormenting you and will end by wiping you out.

You are just going to have to understand Christ's admonition differently. The other cheek means the other side, the other aspect of yourself, in other words, the aspect of the spirit, power and light. That is the side Jesus turned to his tormentors. His whole attitude proclaimed it: "You can imprison my physical body, you can even crucify it, but I'll show you the other side of my being, the indestructible, sublime side, and within three days I'll rebuild my temple!" And he did as he had promised: he showed his other side with the result that the whole world was revolutionized.

Christians, and spiritual people in general, still have a lot to learn and understand. Instead of always letting the forces of darkness and materialistic philosophies get the better of them, they must learn to unite and conquer. They have a habit of saying, "Amen. Amen. So be it..." and accepting whatever gets flung at them. It is high time, now, that they joined forces. They have it in their power to transform the world and restore the Kingdom of God on earth. The time for saying that Jesus taught his followers to turn the other cheek and let themselves be martyred is over, now. In the past that was all right, people could not do otherwise; they were not sufficiently advanced to react divinely. But that argument does not hold water today.

Today we have to look for opportunities to manifest the power of the spirit through our understanding and love, through our every gesture and the whole of our behaviour. This is where true strength lies. Why should men be forever weak, spineless and cowardly? To show that they are Christians? Well, if that were the Christian ideal I should be the first to say that the world will never be rid of evil if we have to rely on a bunch of weaklings like that! No! We have to be strong and mighty, dynamic, active, impetuous, even violent... but on a different level, of course: not physically. If Christ's teaching is not properly understood it is worthless. True Christianity teaches us to be well armed but with another kind of weapon and, when we are attacked, to show that other side, the side that is well armed, not puny and impotent. Up to now no one has ever explained what that "other side" was.

So many things were not properly understood in the past, but the time is now ripe to shed some new light on them so that they can be understood... and there are many other, quite new things, still to be revealed, as well. For nothing is ever stagnant; everything changes and evolves. Jesus himself demonstrated this perfectly, since his teaching constituted a new and different moral law which went much further than the Law of Moses. On several occasions the Gospels tell of how Jesus said: "Ye have heard that it was said by them of old... but I say unto you...." " Let me give you some examples of what I mean: "Ye have heard that it was said... thou shalt not kill: and whosoever shall kill shall be in danger of the judgment. But I say unto you that whosoever is angry with his brother... shall be in danger of the judgment." "Ye have heard that it was said... thou shalt not commit adultery. But I say unto you that whosoever looketh on a woman to lust after her hath committed adultery with her already in his heart." And, again: "Ye have heard that it hath been said... thou shalt not foreswear thyself, but shall perform unto the Lord thine oaths. But I say unto you, Swear not at all." And, finally: "Ye have heard that it hath been said, Thou shalt love thy neighbour and hate thine enemy. But I say unto you, Love your enemies, bless them that curse you... that you may be the children of your Father who is in heaven."

It is obvious, isn't it, that the moral law taught by Jesus was not the same as that of Moses. So why should there not be another, a newer and better moral law, now? Christians will be scandalized by the very idea because they

consider Jesus to be the last and greatest of
God's messengers. According to them there is no
more to be said: no one can add anything to
what Jesus taught. But suppose Christ Himself
were to come and add other notions – for, after
all, everything grows and evolves – the Christians could not prevent it. All those who cling to
the past and have become set and crystallized in
their ways, will be left behind. We are for evolution, for something even more sublime, for the
new life, the new religion which will spread over
the whole world, Christ's true religion which has
never yet been really and truly put into practice.

As long as men still had a primitive mentality, what could they be expected to understand?
Before anything else they at least had to learn
justice, so Moses was sent to teach justice. Later
on, Jesus was sent by Heaven to teach love and
forgiveness. Yes, but why stop there? That is not
all there is. There is something higher. Forgiveness cannot solve all your problems. Suppose,
for example, someone tries to give you a thrash-
ing: is it forbidden to be stronger than he is?
Why shouldn't you grab him by the leg and hold
him up in the air while you tell him: "So, do
you want me to break every bone in your
body?" But you don't do it, of course! You put
him down again, very gently... isn't that much
better?

What kind of Christianity is that if you always have to let yourself be beaten up and tormented? I cannot accept that. You must be strong; stronger than your enemy so that the merest gesture, a glance, a divine vibration flowing through you, is enough to make him feel that you are better than he is. Feeling so small and inferior, he will beg you not to kill him. "Very well, my friend," you reply, "Are you beginning to understand?" And when you put him down he takes to his heels and leaves you in peace. Now, tell me frankly, is it not better to be strong enough to react like that? I think so: much better. But no one has ever dared to envisage the possibility. The very idea seems far too ambitious, but that is exactly what I am interested in doing for you: giving you that ambition. How long it will take you to reach that degree of strength is another matter, but, at least, cultivate the desire. You will never do anything worthwhile in the world if you are always passive, conciliatory, meek and vulnerable... wishy-washy.

There will be no more martyrs in the future. The martyrs of the past have already made the contribution that was asked of them; they have fulfilled their mission. Besides, the main reason for their torments was to enable them to pay off their debts and make good their past misdeeds more rapidly. But once they are free of debt why should they be martyred again? No. In the future there will be many capable of rendering an enemy powerless before he can even get close enough to do them any harm. You may say, "Surely that's an exaggeration? You're going too far!" No, it is not too far. The time has come for human beings to go far, very far: at the moment they are going down a dead-end street.

If you think that what I am saying is too much for you, very well: Stay where you are. Others have more heroic ambitions: they want to be strong, powerful and enlightened. They have no intention of being eternally victimized by the powers of darkness. When people like that are attacked they put up a fight. They know they are not obliged to submit passively until they go under, on the theory that it is "the will of God". When Christians are stupidly submissive the powers of darkness smack their lips in gleeful anticipation! "Ooh!" they say, "These Christians are delicious. So juicy and tender! Let's make a tasty dish out of them!" In other words, by their attitude, Christians actually serve themselves up as a dainty dish for the powers of darkness. Sometimes one gets the impression that that is their only goal in life! Well, if they really want it that way, I will not object. Let them do as they want and nourish the powers of

darkness.... But a true Christian behaves quite
differently: as soon as he sees dark forces coming towards him he throws out a protective
screen of light. And the light dispels the darkness. This is the truly Christian reaction.

Some of you may say, "But one shouldn't
fight. It is written that we shouldn't try to con-
tend with evil." Well, of course, you should not
try to fight evil on its own homeground; it is far
too powerful. You would inevitably lose the battle. But move onto a higher plane; get above it
and from your vantage point in the high realm of
light you can hurl your rockets and bolts of fire.
You will soon see your adversary turn tail and
run! For man has an impregnable fortress within, the territory of light, and this fortress is well
armed with canons and machine-guns that spit
out fire! What is to prevent you from aiming all
that weaponry at your enemies? Why not bom-
bard them with light? You will not kill them
that way; you will not even hurt them. On the
contrary, by driving all the negative and harmful
elements out of their minds and hearts you will
transform them for the better. You are perfectly
within your rights if you do this. But no... people think they have to "behave like Christians"
and, for them, that means letting themselves be
abused and persecuted without reacting because,
they maintain, a Christian must not respond or

pay someone back if he is ill-treated. But the only rule that applies here is that we must not pay him back in kind. You have to find another "coin" in which to pay him, and that is what the "other cheek" is.

Why assassinate someone who is trying to assassinate you? Why not paralyze him, blind him, put him to sleep... or anything else that will put him out of action and prevent him from doing any harm? There are some little comedy sketches based on this idea: We see someone plotting all kinds of dastardly deeds against a family, then along comes a friend of the family who talks so much and so well that the villain is completely bemused by the flow of words. In the end he is hamstrung and helpless. And all that because the family-friend was more intelligent than the villain. So, make no mistake about it, you must defend yourself against an aggressor. Not by the same means as he uses, of course; by other, far more potent means, which you never think of using simply because you do not really believe in their efficacity. In fact, most people have no inkling that they exist.

The Christian community will never get out of the morass it is in if it does not learn to work with divine methods. The very fact that it attributes no spiritual value whatever to the sun is proof enough that it has still not discovered the weapons and means it needs to overcome evil. Let me give you an example: Not only did Jesus tell us to turn the other cheek, he also said we were to love our enemies. Now, this is something very difficult. We cannot even be sure that we really love our friends properly; how shall we ever be able to love our enemies? I assure you; analyse yourselves and you will see: it is the most difficult moral law in the world and we may well wonder where Jesus got it from! Well, I can tell you where he got it: from the sun, of course! Whether you love it or hate it, the sun continues to send you light and warmth. You see? The sun is the only being who has solved the problem: he even loves the wicked and confirmed criminals; he sends them light, warmth and life.

Quite apart from his importance in the physical universe, if you consider the sun only from the moral point of view, he is so great, so truly sublime! Just try and find some human examples of that limitless love. Perhaps you will find some amongst the most highly evolved beings, but they will be few and far between. If you really want to understand the purest moral law, you will have to go and find it in the sun, nowhere else. Other people preach but they never manage to practice what they preach, whereas the sun does not preach, he only practices You will never hear him proclaiming: "I love you. I love all my enemies!" He does not say a word: he just goes on loving every single being. The sun is the only one who can reveal the cosmic moral laws to us and teach us to respect them.

Now, I must tell you a story: Once upon a time there was a young schoolteacher. He was not very big or strong but he was a very intelligent, sensible fellow. One day he was with some of his friends in the village square. One of them, a big hulking fellow who was not very bright, was arguing with our hero about something and when the schoolteacher began to get the better of him with his intelligent arguments, the colossus lost his temper and let fly: one, two... and behold, the poor young teacher flat on his back! Of course, the others laughed and applauded the winner... after all he was a real heavyweight and strength is admirable, isn't it?

Our hero went slowly and sorrowfully home, the laughter and jeers of his friends ringing in his ears. But then, wonder of wonders, when he got home he found his cow had calved and there was a lovely little calf in the meadow. He bent over and stroked it and then he picked it up in his arms and hugged it and forgot all about his humiliation. The next morning, and every morning after that, he would go and pick up the calf and pet it.

This went on for a long time, several months in fact, and the calf was rapidly becoming a full-grown bullock, but the schoolteacher still picked it up without really noticing. Then, one day, he suddenly realized that his muscles had developed enormously and he decided to go down to the village square and see his friends. When he got there, there was the big fellow who had knocked him out, still holding forth and boasting. Going up to him the schoolteacher said, "Do you recognize me?" "I'll say I do," said the bully. "You're the fellow I knocked out!" Without a word our hero stooped and grabbed him by the leg and held him up at arm's length, above his head. "Make your peace with God," he said, "Because I'm going to throw you down and smash you to smithereens!" But of course, the big fellow started to beg for mercy: "Oh, forgive me. Forgive me! I'm sorry I hit you. Don't kill me!" And the teacher replied, "Very well. As long as you're sorry..." and put him gently down on the ground. Of course the bully took to his heels and ran: he was in a hurry to get well away. But the other young men were delighted and cheered our hero who went home victorious, feeling very pleased with himself. So you see, you must never let yourself be vanquished and trodden underfoot because that does not help others to improve. They just go on bullying and misusing their strength and they get no better. If you are too meek and mild it encourages people to take advantage of you.

The Lord demands strength, intelligence, light and power of his servants. So, if you want to overcome difficulties and obstacles and get the better of your enemies you have to practice: see if you cannot find a little calf somewhere in your head and pick it up every day... soon you will be so strong and powerful and full of light that you will be capable of picking up your enemies and holding them up in the air while you tell them: "Say your prayers or there'll be nothing left of you!" This will not kill them nor harm them in any way: you will have nothing on your conscience. This is the truly moral way: instead of killing someone you help him and give him a chance to become wiser, more reasonable, better behaved. In other words your reaction can be an important lesson for him.

Do not try to hide behind weakness. Weakness will not save you and nor will stupidity or laziness. You have to meditate, look for solutions, get yourself in trim and when, one day, you have become as bright and as warm as the sun... well, can anyone touch the sun without burning himself? All ill-wishers will steer clear of you because you will be aflame, symbolically speaking. Sooner or later everyone is obliged to surrender in the face of spiritual strength.

You may say, "Yes, but when your enemy sees that you turn the other cheek he's ashamed and asks you to forgive him." Don't you believe it! On the contrary, it only encourages him. No. Follow the example of that young schoolmaster who picked up his calf every day. As an example there is none better: it is unique. Day and night, for years on end, you will practice and grow stronger and stronger until, one fine day, you can go up to your enemies and say, "Hello, there! Do you recognize me? Now you're going to see something...." And seeing your strength and the light radiating from you they will realize that while they were resting on their laurels you were in training and have become invincible.

There are two ways of reacting (in fact there are three or four, or even ten – but to make things simpler, let's just say there are two): one is with gentleness and the other is with strength. And it is important to know when and how to use them. Very often, when you are feeling depressed, worried or discouraged, it is because undesirable spirits are tormenting you like so many flies, mosquitos, wasps or even snakes. Do you think this is the time for gentleness? Do you think you should let them invade you and feed off you without a word of protest? Not a bit of it! This is the time for a show of strength: show them your force, your inner light with a mere word or a gesture. They will understand and they will have learned a useful lesson. And you can do this every day. Why sit there suffering and feeling sorry for yourself? Show the other side, the side of strength and willpower. Get up and chase them away. Never let negative thoughts and feelings drag on; they will torture you to death.

Is all this clear for you now? It goes a bit against the traditional ideas you have always been taught, perhaps, but that does not matter as long as it is useful and it works! We have to adopt the best and most useful methods instead of hanging on, pointlessly to ineffectual ideas and attitudes. For the time being, of course, you may be a bit scandalized, but in the future you will find yourself forced to adopt this new attitude and you will want to be strong, still stronger, always stronger and stronger without violence, without killing anyone or destroying anything, but strong, invincibly strong, thanks to the light!

So you, too, must begin training to become strong. That is the only way. Practice makes perfect. When war breaks out and we have to fight the powers of darkness will you be ready? To begin with, try to overcome the little enemies within. Knock them out! Stop saying, "I'm a Christian. I don't believe in violence." What weird Christians, indeed! True Christians are knights in armour, Christ's army. They have to be well-armed.

Besides, didn't Jesus himself say, "I came not to send peace, but a sword." And doesn't this mean that Jesus was in favour of violence? It does! But what we have to understand is what kind of violence. Jesus waged war on the powers of darkness, on everything black and vile, with the awe-inspiring power of light, love and wisdom. And what about the sun: what do you think the sun is doing? There is nothing more violent than the sun. Does he ask your permission before making it so hot you have to start taking your clothes off? Does he consult the seeds in the ground before he starts bombarding them with light and heat and forcing them to start growing? The sun is the most violent of beings; in spite of anything you can do he lights up and dispels darkness, he sends you his warmth. There is no room for death in the presence of the sun: he makes everything come alive. The violence of the sun is truly formidable!

In this connection there is a lot that could be said about non-violence as Gandhi taught it. At that particular time and in those particular historical circumstances, it was a magnificent poli cy which enabled the Indians to shake off the yoke of British rule. But, generally speaking, non-violence can be a dangerous policy for a country to adopt, for if it is alone in doing so it runs the risk of being swallowed up by the others.

The philosophy of non-violence becomes the ideal solution only when all mankind decides to embrace it, otherwise there will always be a cruel, egotistical neighbour ready to pounce on the poor, unfortunate bodies who refuse to defend themselves, and wipe them out. Non-violence is an excellent philosophy for someone who is determined to tame his lower nature and who is ready to sacrifice himself so as to advance more rapidly. But it cannot solve the problem of war in the world. A nation that decides not to defend itself will be wiped out in short order, both economically and physically.

So what is needed now is that the philosophy of non-violence become collective, world-wide, universal; that it spread throughout the whole of mankind and no longer exist only in the minds of a handful of idealists. Until and unless non-violence becomes a collective ideal it will be powerless to change anything. How many people who wanted to give an example of selflessness have been sent to their death... and is humanity any the better for it? So the ideal has to spread to the whole world. It is quite possible for a philosophy such as this to be excellent if it is shared by an entire population and dangerous if it remains a purely individual ideal. Although it is true, of course, that even as an individual ideal it still has positive value. All the saints and martyrs, all the heros who sacrificed themselves in the past, come back to earth with great gifts and qualities which they can use to influence others for good. But the fact remains that this question of non-violence will never be satisfactorily resolved until it becomes a universal, world-wide policy.

# 9

## "WATCH AND PRAY"

# I

When mischievous, ill-intentioned entities want to undermine you, the first thing they do is try to get you to make some kind of mistake, and if you fall into their trap you give them the right to infiltrate into you and use your weakness to torment you. But if you resist their wiles and avoid making a false step, they are powerless to break into your inner fortress. In other words, the Devil really only has whatever power you give him by opening your door and letting him in. He does not force his way in, he merely suggests... and it is you who consent. You let certain kinds of thoughts and feelings come in and feed on you, for instance and, at once, finding the door open, the Devil – or, if you prefer: negative forces – slip in.

The Devil owes a great deal of his power to the fact that human beings do not realize that most of the things that seem to them so tantalizing and desirable are simply decoys. Whether it

be the desire to seduce a man or a woman for
one's own, passing pleasure, to eliminate a rival
or lay hands on someone else's property, it always presents itself in glowing colours. And that
is where the snare is hidden: in the fact that, at
first sight, it seems so wonderful. It is a great
mistake to portray the Devil as an object of horror with horns and cloven hoofs, always busy
throwing poor souls into the cauldrons of Hell!
It would be much nearer the mark to portray
him as very handsome, well dressed and charm-
ing, always there wherever pleasure is to be
found, where honours or fortunes are to be won.
In fact he is even invited to tea in the very best
drawing-rooms, for he has impeccable manners,
always in the best of taste.... Obviously, then,
nobody realizes it is the Devil and they succumb
to his charm, which is exactly what he wanted:
it is as though human beings opened a breach in
their own, inner fortress and from then on they
are in the power of the enemy. So it is all-
important to learn to discern the true nature of
the suggestions we receive from the forces of
evil. They are always there, beside us, trying to
convince us with all kinds of enticing promises,
and if we let ourselves be convinced they lay us
waste.

So many people complain of feeling ha-
rassed, tortured and tormented by anxiety. They

do not realize that their distress is the direct result of a mistake they made at some point in the past. It was this mistake that opened their doors to the hostile entities which are now creating havoc within them. For this reason, before you decide to undertake anything at all, take a good look at it to make sure that it is compatible with Divine Law; weigh it up and see what you are likely to lose or gain from it, whether it will make you freer or, on the contrary, tie your hands. Once you have thought it over you can go ahead and act. But at least, before you act, take the trouble to consider all the possible consequences and, above all, be aware that you may run the risk of opening your door to negative influences. Jesus said, "Watch ye and pray!" If you get used to being constantly alert and on your guard, to maintaining a conscious bond with Heaven, you will be protected. The forces of evil may swarm around you, grimacing and threatening, but they will not be allowed in.

Doctors find themselves unable to explain a great many of their patients' problems and try to cure them with chemical or surgical techniques which, naturally, are totally ineffectual: the illnesses are caused by negative forces which have insinuated themselves into these people a long time ago, all unknown to them! Their way of life, their mentality, the feelings they entertained or their general behaviour must have been such as to open the door to the enemy. However, I am perfectly aware that this interpretation will not be accepted or understood. How could the shining lights of the medical profession, in the middle of the 20th century, possibly admit that creatures of the astral world slip into human beings to torment them, feed on them and ultimately cause their ruin? In their opinion it is a question of chemical elements which perturb the correct functioning of the psychic structure. That is perfectly true: it is a question of chemistry. But what science does not know is that these chemical elements have run amok owing to the presence of malicious spirits which their patients have, themselves, attracted. The astral world is teeming with creatures like this, and if human beings, whether culpably or from weakness, open their doors to them, they come swarming in and create havoc.

This reality has been very clearly described in Sacred Scripture and clairvoyants often experience the truth of it. But as most human beings have not developed the spiritual faculties that would enable them to discern the realities of the invisible world, they have worked out a philosophy based exclusively on what can be perceived by our five senses and, of course, the conclusions they draw from this philosophy are bound to be false. But if viruses and bacilli, which are living organisms, can only be detected with the help of a microscope, why not admit the possibility that there could be other, even smaller creatures... too small to be seen by our present-day microscopes. Whichever way you look at it there is not a shadow of doubt that the ravages caused by astral entities are just as devastating as those caused by viruses. No doubt science will, one day, invent instruments which will enable doctors to detect these undesirable invaders. In the meantime, it would be better to admit that they do exist and, above all, to guard against falling into their clutches by allowing reason and intelligence to rule your lives.

I think that if scientists took literature more seriously, instead of thinking it was all a figment of the imagination, they would have already paid much more attention to some of the classical descriptions of psychological cases in which a person is obviously being harried by undesirables. Guy de Maupassant's short story "The Horla", for instance, tells a tale very similar to de Maupassant's own history, for he ended his days in a psychiatric institution, feeling himself the prey of all kinds of evil entities.

In this story, de Maupassant describes how an entity, which he calls the Horla, comes and squats on his chest at night, while he is asleep. It

tries to strangle him and, putting its mouth to
his, sucks his life from him, like a leech. One
morning when he woke up, he noticed that the
water-jug he had filled the evening before was
empty. He did not remember having got up in
the night to drink and thought that, perhaps, he
walked in his sleep. But just to make sure, he decided to experiment: before going to bed he
filled two jugs, one with water and the other with
milk. He wrapped each one in a cloth, tied down
the stoppers and went to bed. When he woke, a
few hours later, the bottles were still wrapped up
and the stoppers tied down, but both bottles
were empty; their contents had been drunk.

Little by little he finds that his will no longer
belongs to him: he wants to get up from his arm-
chair and the Horla prevents him from doing so;
he wants to take the train to Paris, but instead of
telling the cab-driver to take him to the railway
station, he hears his own voice telling him to
drive him home. And finally, one night, he cannot see his own reflection in the mirror: the
Horla, in spite of being almost immaterial, has
put itself between him and his reflection. At that
point he can stand it no longer and tries to find
some way of killing the creature. He ends by setting fire to his own house... which, of course, is
not a very effective solution because one cannot
get rid of these entities by physical means.

Maupassant is not the only writer to tell a tale of this kind for, make no mistake about it, space is teeming with millions of malevolent entities which have sworn to bring mankind to ruin. Of course, there are also billions of luminous entities which are there to help and protect us. But their help and protection can be rendered totally ineffectual if men themselves do nothing to keep on the right path. No Master, no invisible entity can protect you if you persist in living unreasonably. They can instruct and counsel you, they can even influence you to a certain extent by their thoughts and feelings, but if you systematically destroy all their good work by your own carelessness and stupidity, what can they do about it?

The very best forms of protection against undesirables are purity and inner light. When you are shielded by purity and light, mischievous entities cannot get a hold on you, and since you have none of their kind of food to offer them, and they are afraid of light... they leave you alone. This is why, for years and years now, I have been giving you methods by which you can purify yourselves and surround yourselves with an impregnable bulwark of light and colour to ward off evil entities. The intense vibrations of light scatter and disintegrate these creatures. This is why it is so important that you work with light and, by your meditations and prayer, protect your dwelling place by filling every corner of it with light. I use the word "light" but in point of fact it is a question of other entities, beneficial entities. Once they are established in your home they prevent others from coming in. And the same is true of your own person : surround yourself with light.

This does not mean that once you possess a strong aura, an inner fortress of light, you will never be disturbed or attacked again. Unfortunately, as long as we are on this earth we shall never be wholly free from attack and strife. But still, if we are surrounded by a sturdy fence of light it does make things different. Even Initiates are obliged to protect themselves. Even the strongest and most powerful have to take care to build a barrier of light, a circle of flame between themselves and the spirits of evil who try to molest them. And then the weak and ignorant stupidly imagine they need no protection! It is high time you understood the importance, the deep seriousness of all this, otherwise you will be at the mercy of every trend, every influence. From now on, therefore, remember to surround yourself with a circle of light every day.

Some people tell me they trust in talismans for their protection. Well, I believe in the power of talismans, too ; perhaps more than anyone, only my belief is different from theirs. I believe in the protective power of a talisman as long as one lives and works on both the psychic and the physical level in harmony with what it represents, in accord with the virtues and powers it contains, because in that way one nourishes and reinforces its power. But if you count on a talisman and, at the same time, your behaviour and attitudes are in contradiction to all that it represents, after a while it will become ineffectual and die.

A talisman is potent only if you sustain and nurture its potency by the way you live. If it is impregnated with purity, you must live in purity; if it is impregnated with light or strength, you must surround yourself with light or exert yourself so as to enhance its strength, and so on. And it is the same thing for the aura: if you are content to surround yourself with light mentally and do not live a luminous life, your efforts at mental concentration will not be very effective, because you are building up something at one moment and tearing it down the next. It is like those fairy tales, in which the wicked spirits, under cover of night, destroy whatever the young prince or the handsome knight has accomplished during the day. Never forget that, in every case, the only way of accomplishing anything really worthwhile is to improve your way of life.

# II

All that destiny has in store for you can be read in the life you are living today: the direction you give to your thoughts and feelings, the activities which absorb your energies have a determinative influence on your future. If you are attentive and watchful today, you can smooth out the path you will tread in the future. If, on the contrary, you are careless and nonchalant, your future will be strewn with all kinds of useless, even harmful, elements which will hinder your proper development.

All day yesterday you should have been preparing today. And I will give you the secret of how to do so: several times a day, stop and say to yourself, "Now, just a minute, old man! What are you spending all your energies on? What are you aiming for?" Show proof of a little wisdom, at last; show that you have a sense of economy! This in the only way of starting off the following day in the best possible conditions.

The key, the most important key to the problem is always to be vigilant and on the alert, even when you are asleep. Yes: wide awake and on the alert. Why do you think Jesus told his followers to "Watch and pray"? Even spiritual people have never fully understood the importance of this precept. Why be vigilant? It is very fatiguing to be always on the look-out, whereas it is so lovely to sleep, to let yourself go and be mentally and physically lazy! Well, here you have the reason why, in spite of having the whole universe spread out before them, in spite of the sun and the stars, in spite of all the books and all the great Masters who are there to teach them, human beings never get any further. It is because they are asleep... always asleep. You must think about being watchful, therefore, of keeping an eye on yourself, and say to yourself, "Careful, now. I have to prepare for tomorrow by not overloading myself with all kinds of cumbersome material. In my choice of food as well as in my thoughts and feelings I'm going to accept only the most subtle and luminous elements so as to build up my brain, heart and lungs. In this way I shall always be wide awake, alert and dynamic... dynamic even when I'm asleep."

Yes, it is possible. There are different kinds of sleep: some kinds of sleep are sluggish and leaden, a sort of annihilation; whereas in others the brain is in a state of such limpidity, is so lucid and clear that someone can do his best work and be most receptive to instructions at these moments. Now, whatever you do, don't stop reading and meditating in order to sleep! In the first place, if you are not energetic, active and wide-awake prior to sleeping you will never have that kind of "transparent" sleep. If you begin by learning to be vigilant then, when you do sleep, you, nevertheless, remain awake; on another level you hear and understand and act.

The need for vigilance is one of the things you should never forget or neglect. Yes, be watchful in order to prepare for the morrow. Perhaps someone may object, "It seems to me that this contradicts what Jesus said. Several times, in the Gospels, it says that Jesus told his disciples not to worry about the morrow; it would take care of itself." Well, if you think there is a contradiction between the two, you are mistaken. When Jesus told his followers not to take thought for the morrow it was because he saw that human beings were constantly worrying about what the future would bring: whether they would have enough food, a roof over their heads, whether they would be short of money, and so on. Human beings are so absorbed by these material problems that they neglect the most important of all: they abuse their own physical health, they jostle and bully people and things, they break all the laws of love and justice and totally ignore the spiritual dimension. In this way, every day of their lives is littered with unsolved problems and unredeemed faults. All this piles up from day to day until they are buried and crushed beneath it.

So this is why Jesus said not to worry about the morrow: if you take care to do whatever has to be done and to do it correctly each day, the following day will be smooth sailing and you will be free to do whatever you want, while still being careful not to leave a trail of loose ends as you go along. The start of each new day will find you eager and ready, ready to breathe deeply, to study, sing and rejoice... and your whole life will take on marvellous hues of happiness and grace. This is how Jesus' words should be understood. By taking care to do everything correctly today, you provide, indirectly, for tomorrow.

So, do not think about tomorrow. Think about today. If everything is in order today, it will all fall into place tomorrow, too. It is automatic. And as everything is recorded, once you have lived one splendid day, a day of eternal life, it is put on record, it never dies or disappears. It remains very much alive and tends to influence the days that follow so that they will be like it.

Try to live at least one perfect day and it will be contagious: it will influence all the others. It will invite them all to a conference and then it will convince them to follow in its footsteps: to be well-balanced, harmonious and well-ordered. As you have never studied the magical aspect of the question, you may well say, "What difference can one day make? Today was a mess, it's true. But tomorrow will be better!" Well, I hope so. It can be better, on condition that, without further delay, you restore order to the present. Otherwise it will be like one of those games of ninepins you see at a Fair: a ball knocks over one skittle and it, in turn, knocks down all the others.

Many years ago there was a sister who used to come to the Brotherhood meetings. She was a strange kind of person: she had everything anyone could possibly need to be happy in life and, over and above that, she had the light of the Teaching. But she was always somber and anxious-looking. One day, wanting to find out why she was always sad, I asked her some questions and what was my surprise to learn that she was in a perpetual state of worry about what might happen in the future. So many terrible things could happen: accidents, illness, financial disasters and impoverishment! Her whole existence was poisoned because she spent all her waking hours imagining what dreadful things the future might have in store for her! In an attempt to help her, I explained, "Your attitude won't make things any better. On the contrary. It's perfectly true that we can't tell what the future holds, but the best way to avoid all those disasters you're so afraid of, is to try and live a sensible life now, in the present. Instead of poisoning the present by being in a constant frenzy of worry about the future, try to think only of the present moment and make it as good as it can possibly be. In this way you will be building a good future."

It is impossible to build a good future with the building materials of a bad present, for present and future are not two, separate things. If your present is somber and absurd it is no use hoping for a shining future. It is exactly as though you wanted to build a marble palace on a clay foundation. It would not work: the whole thing would fall down. Unfortunately, all these builders – not of cathedrals, but of futures – try to do just that. They do not understand that you cannot build a solid future on a worm-eaten present. So, if you have had a bad day, try at least before you go to bed, to counteract the negative effects by entertaining the best and most luminous thoughts and taking the best possible decisions for the following day. If you do this, those positive thoughts will set to work and, like so many busy little bees, clean and repair everything during the night.

You have come to this Teaching in order to make a new start in life. If you do not do this you will continue to live in chaos and suffering. You will continue to put the blame on everybody else – including God Himself – for all your misfortunes. You will continue to believe that no one recognizes your true worth: you are so just and noble, a person of such integrity; by rights, Heaven and earth should be at your beck and call to satisfy your every whim! It is high time you got rid of all these nonsensical demands on others and embarked on a wholly new life. Oh, it is not easy, I know. The past is still there, clinging on to you. And just as the future is tied to the present, so too the present is tied to the past. But there is one big difference: we have it in our power to fashion the future whereas we can do nothing to change the present. It is the outcome of the past.

"Watch and pray." To watch means, of course, not to fall asleep, but on the spiritual, not on the physical level. We have to be awake and watchful in our minds at every instant of the day and night if we want to be aware of the presence of impure, harmful elements or currents, especially if we want to avoid them. Anyone who fails to be on the alert leaves himself open to every kind of danger. There is nothing worse than to go through life with your eyes closed. Keep your eyes open at all times so as to be aware of what is going on in yourself, so as to be in a position to identify the different currents, the different states of mind, all the different thoughts and feelings that flow through you. Only those who live with their eyes open can comprehend that inner world and retain their freedom, instead of being at the mercy of whatever force or entity comes along. A sleeping man is an obvious target for a surprise attack! So be on the watch!

And now, what does the "pray" mean in that phrase: "Watch and pray"? When you have "watched", in other words, when you have looked into yourself and seen what is going on, you are going to have to intervene, to get directly involved in order to get rid of certain elements, introduce others and establish yourself as master of the situation so as to prevent your enemies from getting in and laying waste to everything. That is what is meant by "pray". To pray is to find a remedy, to improve a situation, and the most effective way of doing this is to establish a bond with Heaven. The human brain is like a radio or television set: it can tune in to all kinds of different transmitters operating on different wavelengths. All you have to do with a transistor radio is to choose the programme you want and turn a little knob until you get it: music, a news bulletin or whatever you want. Well, you can do this with your own inner transistor, too... and if you push the wrong button you may get nothing but static and clamour or a blast of music straight from Hell! When this happens, switch to another station. It is as easy as can be; all you need do is to use your mind or your imagination to tune in to a programme from Heaven.

To pray is simply to push the right button and tune in to the shortest and most rapid wavelengths which put you in communication with the Lord God, and by so doing you change your own vibrations. To pray is to trigger a positive, luminous, divine movement within.

Amongst all the treasures of wisdom the Initiates have given to men, none is more prècious than prayer, for anybody and everybody can pray, even the simplest, most ignorant of men. Look at a child: from the depths of his innocent little heart he screams, "Mummy". His cry is a prayer to his mother and he knows his mother will answer him. And if you too ask with the same candour, innocence and purity as a child, your prayer will be answered. As soon as you begin to pray an invisible army gathers round you, the soft rustle of angels' wings can be heard and the spirits of darkness who were plotting your downfall disappear in a flash: they know only too well that if they stay they will be tormented, consumed by fire, struck down by lightning. They fear only one thing, these undesirable entities: light. So, whenever you are in difficulty or danger, your first reaction should be to establish communication with your Creator and turn on all the lights within. If you do this you will effectively disarm or drive away all those creatures from below who were threatening you.

Some people may say that they pray but without result. Perhaps this very simple but effective method can help: when you want to pray call up the image in your mind of the multitude of spirits throughout the world who, each in his own sphere, is concentrating all his powers of thought on his Creator. And then, in your mind, join with them in prayer. Your voice will no longer be alone and solitary in the wilderness of life; you will be united to all those other voices raised to Heaven in prayer. This kind of prayer is always heard, because of the community, and you yourself will benefit from it. If your prayer is not heard, now, it is because you are praying alone. The secret is to join forces with all the other people who are praying, for at every moment of the night or day, there is always somebody at prayer, somewhere in the world.

**By the same author :**
*(translated from the French)*

## Izvor Collection

**By the same author**
*(translated from the French)*

**'Complete Works' Collection**

**Brochures :**
*New Presentation*

*Editor-Distributor*

**Editions PROSVETA S.A. – B.P. 12 – 83601 Fréjus Cedex (France)**

---

*Distributors*

**AUSTRIA**
MANDALA
Verlagsauslieferung für Esoterik
A-6094 Axams, Innsbruckstraße 7

**BELGIUM**
PROSVETA BENELUX
Van Putlei 105 B-2548 Lint

N.V. MAKLU Somersstraat 13-15
B-2000 Antwerpen

VANDER S.A.
Av. des Volontaires 321
B-1150 Bruxelles

**BRAZIL**
NOBEL SA
Rua da Balsa, 559
CEP 02910 - São Paulo, SP

**BRITISH ISLES**
PROSVETA Ltd
The Doves Nest
Duddleswell Uckfield,
East Sussex TN 22 3JJ

Trade orders to :
ELEMENT Books Ltd
Unit 25 Longmead Shaftesbury
Dorset SP7 8PL

**CANADA**
PROSVETA Inc.
1565 Montée Masson
Duvernay est, Laval, Que. H7E 4P2

**GERMANY**
PROSVETA DEUTSCHLAND
Höhenbergweg 14
D - Bad Tölz

**HOLLAND**
STICHTING
PROSVETA NEDERLAND
Zeestraat 50
2042 LC Zandvoort

**HONG KONG**
HELIOS – J. Ryan
P.O. BOX 8503
General Post Office, Hong Kong

**IRELAND**
PROSVETA IRL.
84 Irishtown – Clonmel

**ITALY**
PROSVETA Coop. a r.l.
Cas. post. 13046 – 20130 Milano

**LUXEMBOURG**
PROSVETA BENELUX
Van Putlei 105 B-2548 Lint

**NORWAY**
PROSVETA NORDEN
Postboks 5101
1501 Moss

**PORTUGAL**
PUBLICAÇÕES
EUROPA-AMERICA Ltd
Est Lisboa-Sintra KM 14
2726 Mem Martins Codex

**SPAIN**
ASOCIACIÓN PROSVETA ESPAÑOLA
C/ Ausias March nº 23 Principal
SP-08010 Barcelona

**SWITZERLAND**
PROSVETA
Société Coopérative
CH - 1808 Les Monts-de-Corsier

**UNITED STATES**
PROSVETA U.S.A.
P.O. Box 49614
Los Angeles, California 90049

**VENEZUELA**
J.P. Leroy
Apartado 51 745
Sabana Grande
1050 A – Caracas

PRINTED IN FRANCE IN SEPTEMBER 1989
EDITIONS PROSVETA Z.I. DU CAPITOU,
B.P.12, 83601 FRÉJUS CEDEX
FRANCE

– N° d'impression : 1764 –
Dépôt légal : September 1989
Printed in France